"For nearly 50 years, Jerry Daley has been on point regarding the Great Commission. Making disciples has been his passion, and his commitment to it has been sustained and fruitful. This is not a theory book, but one born of a practitioner that provides needed wisdom and insight on how to go about 'making disciples that make disciples.' As you read this book, you'll not only walk with Jerry in his journey to make disciples, but you'll also receive an impartation to go and do likewise."

Rich Kao
Senior Pastor, Five Stones Church, Vancouver, BC

"Before Jesus left this earth He gave us one job, one simple job—make disciples. Jerry Daley is a master of the art of personal discipleship. In 34 years of full-time ministry, I have not met his equal. Get a cup of coffee, find a comfortable chair, open your journal, and prepare to join the journey."

Michael Fletcher
Senior Pastor, Manna Church, Fayetteville, NC
and leader of mPact Churches network

"It is my honor and privilege to have been in relationship with Jerry Daley for more than 40 years. During these years he has been a mentor, pastor, co-laborer, and most of all, friend. I was an Army chaplain on active duty at Fort Bragg when Jerry took me on as a disciple. I experienced every step he describes in this book. Jerry prayed with me, encouraged me, challenged me, and even rebuked me at times. Ultimately he helped me to pursue my heart's desire: to know Christ and make Him known. Every person who comes to faith in Jesus is called to be a disciple—and called to make disciples. This book will make this point clear, and more than that, it will help you know what it means to be a disciple and how you can fulfill your divine destiny as a disciple-maker.

Dr. Ron Crews
'red
Executive Director, (ʾrty

D1414360

"If you are serious about discipleship, you must read *Doing Life With*. Jerry has been discipling those who have gone on to become leaders in the Kingdom for half a century. The complete process— from finding your first disciples to seeing them reproduce their life in another—it's all here! This book is written for the heart, not the head. No pre-formed strategies are given, no 10-step program laid out. This book is about life-on-life discipleship, reproducing what God has given you in others. The way Jesus did it. This is Jerry's story, told as only Jerry can tell it. The book is practical, biblical, and filled with experience! If you are investing your life in others, put this at the top of your reading list!"

Patrick Lai
Founder of Open Network
Author of Tentmaking *and* Business for Transformation

"Jerry Daley brings his significant experience in planting churches, making disciples, and strong Christian theology to benefit those seeking to more effectively spread God's Word. He brings a practitioner's view, humor, and personal stories to the universal challenge of mobilizing believers as active disciples."

Thad Wolfe
Lt. General USAF Retired
Colorado Springs, CO

"I had the privilege of being mentored by Jerry Daley for over twenty years. Other than my parents, no one was used by God to shape my life and ministry like Jerry. *Doing Life With* is more than a book; it is Jerry's life message. He has lived and breathed a lifestyle of making disciples and training leaders for the 44 years I have known him. This book is not just a handbook on discipleship. It is also a primer on how to practically apply the great doctrines of the Christian faith to every area of our lives. Whether you have just begun making disciples or you have been making disciples for decades, this book provides a powerful roadmap for success."

Jim Laffoon
International Leadership Team, Every Nation Churches & Ministries

DOING

LIFE

WITH

JERRY DALEY

Jerome Daley Apostolic Foundation
200 Sage Road
Chapel Hill, NC 27514

www.JerryDaley.com

Scripture quotations, unless otherwise noted, are taken from the New American Standard Bible®, copyright © 1960, 1962, 1963, 1968, 1971, 1972, 1973, 1975, 1977, 1995 by The Lockman Foundation. Used by permission. (www.Lockman.org)

Some of the anecdotal illustrations in this book are true to life and are included with the permission of the persons involved. All other illustrations are composites of real situations, and any resemblance to persons living or dead is coincidental.

Cover design: Josh Daley & Daniel St. Armand

Images: Graphicriver.net

Interior layout: Jerome Daley

ISBN-13: 978-1530944996

ISBN-10: 1530944996

Rev. 170225

Contents

JOIN THE COMMUNITY

A Private Facebook Group

If you are reading this book, then you share my passion. You are a Christ-follower who wants to help others follow Jesus too. You want to be a disciple who disciples—and you're getting ready to learn how to do that more easily and more effectively than ever before.

So here's the thing. You're not in this alone. We are part of a larger discipleship community, so let's inspire, encourage, and equip one another. This is meant to be fun, so join our community of like-minded folks, everyday Christians who want to change the world like Jesus. With Jesus. And with one another.

You're invited! Join our private Facebook group by using this link: **www.facebook.com/groups/doinglifewith**.

Welcome aboard!

Jerry Daley

PREFACE

Imagine something with me for a moment. We are sitting in with the Father, Son, and Holy Spirit and watching them experience community together. Observing how they relate to one another...how they talk, serve, and simply are with each other. Mind-boggling thought, isn't it?

Love has its origin right there in the heart of God. And it is love that finds joy in blessing another. We can only dream about the exquisite fellowship experienced within the Trinity as they continually express love, affection, and delight in one another. It is truly who they are.

So it should come as no surprise then that the Lord draws Abraham to Himself and shares what's on His heart—Father to son— "I will bless you, and make your name great." Wow, what an offer! But then watch what happens next: "...and so you shall *be* a blessing." Can you see God inviting Abraham to share the Godhead love-experience so that he too might become a source of blessing to all the families of the earth? (Genesis 12:2-3) Blessing is what love does.

Every human parent gets this at an intuitive level (except when their humanity has been damaged by the absence of love). We love our children. We want extraordinary amounts of good in their lives. In short, we want to bless them. Our parental love shows itself in wanting to nurture and protect, to see them grow and prosper, and ultimately for them to enter into and extend these blessings to others.

As a parent I want my three children to have the best relationships, the best marriages, healthy bodies, excellent character, and meaningful jobs so that they can benefit others. I want my children to become who they really are and fulfill the design for which they were created. We all want our kids to experience the full measure of blessing in their lives.

So look again at Abraham's invitation to blessing. Suppose we recast this man as the disciple of *The One Who Comes to Bless*. It's a different way to look at both Abraham and God, but I think it fits. God calls Abraham out, dumps unexpected blessing on his life, and then challenges him to become a blessing to others.

Now think about Jesus. He came to release captives, recover sight, set the oppressed free, and bring favor (Luke 4:18-19). Sounds like blessing, doesn't it? I like to think of it as redemption reframed. The Father sent the Son to remove curses and bring people into His goodness. He wants the absolute best for every person! Including you.

No story represents this truth better than Jesus' famous description of the Father looking for the return of his "prodigal son." He is patiently, longingly waiting for the return of a child broken by sin and shame. When he catches a glimpse of his bedraggled boy trudging along the road in disgrace, He races to meet him, arms outstretched, falling on his neck with tears and kisses and shouts of joy! The effusiveness of the Father's welcome catches me off guard. Even after many readings, it still gets me.

Above all things, the desire to bless is manifest in a desire *to be with*! A yearning for togetherness and deep-hearted fellowship. No wonder then that God comes as Emmanuel—the "God with." He Himself comes to be with us in an unprecedented display of passion and humility. He chooses to walk with us through every step and bend of life.

Mark described Jesus' call of the early disciples this way: "He appointed twelve, so that they would be *with Him*" (Mark 3:14). And years later, even as He was leaving them He promised, "Surely I am *with you* always" (Matthew 28:20). The incarnation was the Father's ultimate blessing for His children, and it was this "with-ness" that profoundly marked the disciples. The religious leaders that persecuted the early church "recognized them as having been *with Jesus*" (Acts 4:13). It is His being with us that marks us forever.

Why are we talking about love and blessing and God being with us? Because we really can't (or shouldn't) understand Jesus' commission to disciple others outside of this context. There are lots of potential motivations for making disciples, some better and some less good, but I have yet to find a better reason than to bless others and equip them to extend that blessing even further. As I see it, this is the big story of redemption history…and our place in it.

For this reason I think of disciple-making as helping others to indulge in the rich, free blessings that come from following the One that our Father sent. He would not rest until He found us, restored us, and joined Himself to us. Amazingly Jesus called us "brothers" (Hebrews 2:11). Why? Because we all have the same Father!

INTRODUCTION

The Discovery of "With"

"Son, you can do a lot of things well, but being a preacher is not one of them."

It had only been eight days since I had been ambushed by the Holy Spirit and drawn, along with my wife Nan, into a glorious saving encounter with Jesus. This Saturday morning I awakened to an overpowering realization—the knowledge that God was calling me to preach. That driving the Great Commission forward was now my personal calling. Not optional. Not negotiable.

The presence that surrounded me that morning in April of 1966 hung upon me for hours like an invisible cloak, and when it lifted, a permanent imprint remained upon my soul. An unshakable conviction that the world needed a revolution of grace, a quiet explosion that would rock it to its core and bring it to its knees before its Creator.

As an Air Force pilot fresh out of flight training, I immediately shared this new-found mission with my father-in-law, an Air Force Major General. He had always believed in me and had welcomed me warmly into his family when Nan and I married several years before. Without any demeaning intent, his response was heartfelt: "Son, you can do a lot of things well, but being a preacher is not one of them."

I couldn't disagree. Public speaking had never been my strong suit. I had a hard time imagining it myself: *Jerry Daley, preacher.* It was a strange thought! But then, it wasn't my thought; it was God's and it had come with unquestionable clarity. Ready or not, my path was set, and over the coming years I discovered how God's voice would speak through me.

A DIVINE STRATEGY

The Spirit of God has a way of raising up voices that have a prophetic edge: Robert Coleman was such a man. Fifty years ago he authored a simple but revolutionary book entitled *The Master Plan of Evangelism*. Reading it today, although the language is dated, the truths are timeless and striking. It resonates powerfully because the strategies belong to God Himself.

Our modern lives are so packaged in serial change that we aren't always prepared to hear the voice of the Holy Spirit in fifty-year-old words. Truth is, the ideas go back at least two thousand years, to Jesus as He walked the ancient roads of the Middle East. As a result of Jesus' approach to disciple-making, the gospel exploded across a nation, a continent, and ultimately the known world. *How well have we stewarded that approach today?*

Over the centuries, various groups have rediscovered Jesus' priority on relational discipleship with dramatic results. But the lulls between those explosions have been long and dark; people have remained captive while the powerful means of their liberation sat by untouched. We have everything we need—it was given to us by Jesus Himself. It's time to put it into action and *do life with!*

Disciples making disciples defines the potential of the church to change the world.

RECENT GAINS

Allow me to offer a perspective on how the church has made remarkable strides in the last generation: A veritable flood of leadership books occupy our shelves. Many new churches are growing at phenomenal rates. New church networks are appearing regularly. We see a proliferation of how-to-build systems for reaching a new cross-section of Americans. A brand new generation of young church planters is sincere, nonreligious, kingdom-minded, authentic, smart, and hard-working. Truly, amazing things are being done.

This is important to recognize because the church is Jesus' number one love—it's His Bride. There is much to applaud in the church today. And because of God's love for the church, it is helpful for us— along with Robert Coleman—to drop a plumb line into this community and offer alternatives to some of the assumptions and practices often taken for granted.

CULTURE SHIFT

Here's where Jesus started: He declared, "I will build *My* church" (Matthew 16:18). This is His job, His initiative, His idea. Fortunately, He also makes our job explicit: "Go, make disciples, baptizing them and teaching them to observe all that I commanded you; and lo, I am with you always, even to the end of the age." (Matthew 28:19-20). Further, He says that *the lifestyle of disciple-making uniquely links us to His presence.* This is no small point! This means that every Christ-follower is meant to live with a disciple-making mission as the framework of life, whatever our particular profession.

We all agree with this, but here's the rub. It's easy to call ourselves "church planters" (which I do myself) and set our primary focus there—on building authentic faith gatherings—rather than on making disciples. Disciples who make disciples. These two excellent goals are not mutually exclusive, of course. But because large group events are more visible than one-on-one work, it's easy to get consumed in the former to the neglect of the latter without really being aware of the shift.

Here's a simple way for all of us to run a quick self-assessment: how much time, energy, and money do we devote to building organizational systems, hiring consultants, and designing high-tech worship centers...and how much time, energy, and money are we devoting to the personal transformation of those we lead? Maybe even more to the point, how are we doing at creating a discipleship culture and observing a Christ-centered discipleship explosion? These are questions that I think Jesus would gently invite us to consider, to see where we can maintain our commitment to the large community experience while also exploring ways to be more intentional and more relational in the way we approach discipleship.

In the name of efficiency it's enticing to relegate discipleship to systems for handling large numbers. And that can be a legitimate starting point. But the kind of discipleship that Jesus practiced requires more than group training; it calls for something much more up-close-and-personal. To be honest, "launch teams" and "dream teams" are more sexy than life-on-life discipleship. Spiritual growth and transformation occasionally happen as the result of a highly-motivated personal pursuit, but more often they occur when *being pursued*...and as spiritual shepherds, this pursuit lies at the heart of our commission.

The transparency and sincerity of the Willow Creek Church leadership makes this need both clear and compelling. Their *Reveal* study, first reported in 2007, disclosed that while they had succeeded in attracting large crowds of the unchurched at unprecedented levels of success and inviting them into the Christian community, they had fallen severely short in deepening the life of faith for many others. This was a classic case of going wide but not deep...and that same danger haunts us all in the modern church.

MEASURING SUCCESS

Now let's dig a little deeper. Most of us wind up placing the vast majority of our budget, personnel, and attention on the Sunday morning event (which sometimes spills into Saturday night or Sunday afternoon with multiple services). The impact of this orientation is a culture more characterized by "Come" than "Go." So how can we get better at both?

Along with our efforts in leadership development, how can we get better at replicating the Christ-life in individual lives? If we succeed in expanding the organization but build that growth upon a base of shallow spirituality, what have we really achieved? Somehow we must avoid the imbalance of merely going big and think that we have achieved our mission.

Coleman points out that Jesus chose His *men* before He started His *meetings*. And the closer He got to the cross, the more time He spent with His disciples. This is not inconsequential. It speaks clearly and powerfully to His priorities.

How many people did Jesus have in His congregation? Only 120 showed up for Pentecost, not a figure that would impress most leaders today. Listen to Coleman speak to the church 50 years ago—and how it resonates today:

Most of the evangelistic efforts of the church begin with the multitudes under the assumption that the church is qualified to conserve what good is done.

The result is our spectacular emphasis upon numbers of converts, candidates for baptism, and more members for the church, with little or no genuine concern manifested toward the establishment of these souls in the love and power of God, let alone the preservation and continuation of the work (p. 33).

AN UNBALANCED SYSTEM

Coleman's point is bold, maybe even offensive to some. But it's always healthy to humble ourselves before a challenging word and ask God where He might want to fine-tune us. As we do, let's consider where most of our spiritual leaders get their training. Many current senior pastors, church planters, and church staff were not themselves personally discipled. The seminary has become the main path to senior church leadership, and this educational model is built primarily upon a classroom environment for transmitting knowledge, reading books, and taking exams. While these are valuable tools, they are no replacement for the ancient practice of apprenticeship.

Patrick Lai, a leader in the B4T (business for transformation) movement and former overseer with the missions agency Frontiers, has worked overseas for over thirty years. He says this: "Nearly all the new workers the mission sent me over the years had never been discipled. I found I had to disciple them first, and only then they were ready to reach others."

Because most modern leaders were not apprenticed by a role model and father figure, there is a widespread assumption that the church will accomplish its mission by using some adaptation of the classroom method they received in seminary. So while there is no lack of desire in today's church to accomplish its mission, we often observe a misdirection of attention. In short, it's easy to find ourselves measuring the wrong things.

Often it is we leaders ourselves who are frustrated yet know of no other solution than to work harder, read more books, and innovate more spectacularly in hopes of becoming more effective. Yet if our metrics are wrong, then we cannot succeed with the Great Commission.

Here's the other limitation of the seminary system: since many of our current leaders were not apprenticed, not trained by personal relationship with a role model, they often do not know how to disciple or apprentice another person. Their default methods tend more towards knowledge than relationship...and this approach cannot accomplish (except by accident) the kingdom results we observe in Jesus' day.

Today we are facing two fundamentally different strategies for changing the world for Christ: a conversion focus and a discipleship focus. And it's all too easy to get preoccupied with the one to the detriment of the other. Let's consider for a moment the problem that exists in how one defines what it takes to become a Christian.

DEFINING "CHRISTIAN"

I was recently having a Bible study with a friend who considers himself to be a Christian but has no fruit in his life. He doesn't belong to a church, is not baptized, does not read his Bible, and has no knowledge of what Jesus taught. Listen to his recent comment: "I believe in Christ as my Savior. Isn't that all that is required to be a Christian?" He felt certain I would answer affirmatively; instead, I believe the Holy Spirit gave me a more accurate answer.

"No, Jesus never used the word Christian. He only spoke of disciples." In fact, the people who invented the term Christian were unbelievers (Acts 11:26). Similarly, in the 60s we were labeled "Jesus Freaks" by those who mocked the faith...and we relished the term. Biblically, a believer is *someone who believes in Jesus so as to follow Him and obey Him.* When our following of Jesus personally is lacking, our believing in Jesus loses the essential requirements of commitment and surrender to Christ's lordship (Matthew 7:21; John 14:15).

Once we subtract authentic discipleship from the definition of being a Christian, the strategy for "reaching the world for Christ" gets fundamentally altered, as we can now observe. I think we can do better...and must do better if this lies at the core of our divine commission.

RECLAIMING THE PLAN

Jesus defined the disciple-making process in very few words: "Teaching them to observe all that I commanded you" (Matthew 28:20). The process is extraordinarily simple—He teaches you, and in turn you impart that foundation to the life of another. It's ancient and low-tech, and this simplicity often gets lost in the complexity of modern leadership for several reasons.

- It means spending a lot of personal time with a few people on a regular basis. This often feels inefficient.

- It means operating in a high level of transparency, personal accountability, authenticity, and humility. This can feel risky.

- It means adapting your teaching style to the unique needs of those being discipled. This can feel labor-intensive.

If, as people often say, "Time is money," then the bulk of your discipleship "budget" must be spent pouring into the lives of men in one-on-one relationships...or in very small groups. Not surprisingly, this is the way God disciples us—within the context of a personal relationship.

When we rely more upon our leadership gifts than our personal time with Jesus and the Holy Spirit's guidance, something crucial gets lost. And Jesus' discipleship strategy wasn't just for leaders; it was for every man, woman, and teen—a strategy that allows us to grow rapidly in our relationship with God by personally investing in another person. It's brilliant! Creating maturity and multiplication at the same time.

So many have invested in my life! The book that follows is the sum of five decades of my own discipleship journey in Christ—showcasing the results of other leaders' personal training of me as well as the theory and practice I've had to learn the hard way. Discipling other leaders has become my greatest passion, so this book contains both the content and the strategy for multiplying God's life in others— at least the version that has been entrusted to me.

On a practical note, my discipleship attention is focused entirely upon men (and my wife's upon women), but I have included both masculine and feminine pronouns in the book since discipleship truths apply equally to women and men.

Today we have the opportunity, both men and women, to reclaim the same revolutionary power for life-on-life cultural transformation that the early church experienced. It's not complicated, it's not expensive, and it's not technology-dependent. It doesn't have to be invented or innovated. It just has to be noticed, embraced, and activated for us to experience early-church results.

The dynamite is in place. The explosive potential of Jesus' approach to disciple-making is all there. It's time to light the fuse.

ONE

Getting Started
It's Easier Than You Think

Gold's Gym is my current "fishing pond" (Matthew 4:19). I have something in common with these people. They are my tribe—I like them, I understand them, and I'm their pastor. They don't know that, but I am. Really I'm just a guy on the lookout for a conversation, a name, some rapport, a connection. It's fun to watch for little opportunities to ask a question, to encourage, to listen, or to enjoy someone. Who can resist being liked?

For some months I watched Troy from afar. The best trainer in the gym, he was liked by the ladies. But I had a suspicion that he was on God's radar. Interestingly enough, my own trainer left Gold's, and I ended up being assigned to who-do-you-think? Troy.

Mark it down: When someone is teaching you, he or she is in a confident position, feels secure, and is vulnerable to you taking an interest and asking questions. This is a Holy Spirit atmosphere. I didn't have to "do" anything with Troy. The relationship felt natural, just being a friend to him. Questions led to suggestions about faith.

Okay, I was a little bummed that I didn't personally get to introduce Troy to Jesus, but I was thrilled when he shared his new faith with me! I savored the moment with him, and soon his questions took us right into biblical discipleship. It was easy and natural.

Soon we were meeting together outside of Gold's, for lunch and then for Bible study at his house. Then Troy began inviting other men to study the Bible at his home. The new Troy created quite a sensation in the gym! The change was dramatic, and soon many began to feel God's love coming from an unexpected source. Now Troy is a pastor at Gold's. In fact, there is a steadily growing number of pastors there. A band of pastors in a gym—imagine that.

Getting started as a disciple-maker may sound intimidating, but it's meant to be the most natural thing in the world. As in my engagement with Troy, it didn't take any great theological insight to establish the connection; it just took paying attention and seizing the opportunity to be a friend. This is the essence of "doing life with."

This kind of intentionality in friendship—whether a person doesn't know Christ yet, or is simply new in his faith—opens the door to discipling relationships. What we want is to build a community of men and women who care for one another, help each other know God, and learn how to live a kingdom life.

You don't need an academic degree for this. Jesus' plan is to use you as a "2nd grader" to help a "1st grader" in his or her faith. That means all you need is to know just a bit more about God than the person you're discipling...and have a heart to help people grow. Know anyone who could use some encouragement or friendship? I'm guessing you do.

It is our mindsets that need to change more than anything. We must dismantle all those "old tapes" and old images of what discipleship is about in order to embrace a simple discipleship approach that fits you: your personality, your gifts, and your journey.

Once this happens, it's time to be on the lookout for those people the Holy Spirit is preparing and putting in your path. Some will be obvious, others less so. There are many around you in church who would love some help growing in Christ, but they don't know what they need and they don't know you are available.

Showing interest in people is powerful stuff. Most likely, the people you meet don't encounter this every day—not at work, not in the neighborhood. Conversations tend to stay safe and superficial. Even at church, people often don't know how to ask for help in their spiritual life. Be looking for someone with whom you click.

Who will you be for this person? You will be a sponsor, helping someone succeed. You'll become someone's cheerleader, and that person will become accountable to you in an informal relationship that most people do not offer, men with men and women with women.

These kinds of connections are usually pretty natural. If you are a mother with young children, you might easily connect with another mother. If you're a guy, maybe you like to play racquetball or golf or go to the firing range. I like to work out, so I go to the gym.

Once the initial connection is made, schedule a time to go out for lunch or coffee. Initiate. Be curious. Listen for his story, what she wants for her future, where he is in his spiritual journey. Invite a work colleague to a concert. Find out where he or she has a felt need and do what you can to assist.

Maybe she's had a bad experience with church. Just ask questions and listen. It's therapeutic for people to talk about their experiences with someone who cares. Many have dysfunctional family situations and need a safe place to talk. Find out if your friend is experiencing God's love on a regular basis. Usually not...and if not, that's the place to start.

After you've listened, then share some of your own story. Your transparency models the depth of relationship you're after and invites him to reciprocate. Eventually invite him to study the Bible or a book on a relevant point of interest. Maybe you'll want to study key parts of the gospel of John or a topical book that relates to a particular season of life.

You might be surprised that I don't immediately invite a person of interest to church. Why? Because this can come across more like recruiting than caring. If the person is not in a life-giving church, you might eventually invite her to a study group that offers something in which she has expressed an interest—handling finances, child training, marriage enrichment, knowing God, etc. This makes it easy for her to join your group without having to make a larger commitment. That may come later, or it may not.

There are many ways to begin to disciple a person. Here are some that my wife has used at different times:

- After making a friendship connection she might suggest that they read a book together and meet to discuss it over tea.

- She has used regular running or walking as a point of connection, which then becomes a chance to share about how to do life.

- She has invited younger women into a small group to study a relevant book, and this becomes the touch point that leads to talking about devotions, relationships, attitudes, etc.

As you begin to do this, eventually some will invite you into their lives. For my part I have used different formats:

- Businessmen meeting regularly for lunch.

- College students meeting once a week to share their spiritual journeys.

- High school students gathering to learn the basics of following Christ.

- I have met with many men one-on-one for coffee, for lunch, for walks, and for Bible study.

Before we go any further, let's take a look at one of the simplest and most effective discipleship tools that I have used for many years.

THE FOUR QUESTIONS

These four questions have a way of opening people's hearts and giving you access to the crucial matters of their heart. They can be used more formally—such as in a written report that a disciple emails periodically—or very informally, just woven into the flow of conversation.

Question 1: *What is the state of your soul?*
This question asks someone to pause long enough to assess, *Where am I? What emotions am I experiencing? Am I confused, anxious, fearful, peaceful, excited, disappointed, discouraged, angry, insecure, sad, regretful, pleased, frazzled, lonely, determined, ashamed, curious, restless, hopeless, satisfied, or happy?*

I recently taught a discipleship course in which I had my students practice recognizing and labeling their emotions. Typically, people experience a host of emotions every day but have not yet learned to tag them. When you learn how to name the feeling, it's easier to invite Jesus into what you are experiencing.

My friend Bill likes to ask, "Who here would say that you're under a heavy load?" I always smile when I watch him going there with a group because I know what's coming next. "If you're under a heavy load, it means you're under the wrong end. Jesus promised, 'My burden is light'" (Matthew 11:30). Right. But what if you're under a heavy load yet have not noticed it yourself? Learning to recognize and tag these pesky emotions is almost an art form.

I frequently ask myself in my journal, "What emotions have I experienced in the last 24 hours?" (If you want some help with this, check out the list of emotions in the Appendix.) It's not unusual for me to discover that I blew past feelings that were significant but just hadn't noticed. This is simply another way of asking myself the original question, *What is the state of my soul?*

I laughingly tell men, "Okay, you and your wife are driving along when she breaks the silence with, 'What are you thinking?' An awkward moment goes by, and you say, 'Nothing.' Hmm. How does one think nothing?" Interpretation: We men aren't used to asking ourselves questions like this.

It is amazing how quickly I can get below the surface with a new disciple by teaching him how to use this question.

Question 2: *What is God doing in your life?*
If I come into your house and you are remodeling your kitchen, you won't have to tell me; the mess speaks for itself. Learning to ask this question has a way of tuning us into something God intends to change in our souls.

It makes all the difference in soul-remodeling if you sense what God is doing. This allows you to cooperate with Him and accelerate the process. Maybe He is...

- Working on your patience.

- Inviting you to go to bed earlier so you can meet Him in the morning.

- Helping you recognize and get help for anger.

- Spotlighting worry. Anxiety. Performance-based living.

- Getting rid of shame. Teaching you about faith.

Since God never condemns us, we are learning to be transparent with Him and with a trusted friend. This is how spiritual growth works.

Question 3: *What is God saying to you?*
There may be a connection between what God is doing in your life and what He is saying to you—but not necessarily. It's crucial that we grow in our ability to distinguish His voice, as they say, "up close and personal" (John 10:27).

Here's an example. Let's say that God is working on your marriage relationship as a husband or wife. There are a number of things He could be saying to you:

- Encouraging you.

- Giving you ideas of how to serve your spouse.

- Showing you something you need to discuss.

- Highlighting something to celebrate.

One thing we know: Jesus has promised that His "sheep" hear His voice (John 10:4). We also know that He has turned this job over to the Holy Spirit—to teach, to bring to our remembrance, to encourage, to nudge, to caution, and to restrain. He is always reminding us to pay attention, listen up, and stay tuned.

Question 4: *What are your questions about God, life, or ministry?*
This broad question obviously opens the door to any topic that might be on your friend's (disciple's) mind. How rare is it for someone to have a friend to trust with spiritual questions?

What we are doing with these four questions is simply walking alongside a man or woman in the journey of life. It is the power of "being with," and it is a priceless gift. Jesus promised that when we learn from Him and share with someone else, we will experience His presence in a powerful way (Matthew 28:20).

You can also use these same questions in a less formal way if the friendship (discipleship) is in a less-formal stage. For example, instead of asking, "What is the state of your soul?" you could ask, "Well Bob, how are you doing with God?"

In unusual settings and yet in a very natural way, I often ask, "May I pray for you?" It may surprise some, but I'm never turned down! There is an atheist at my gym who wants me to pray for him...just not publicly. This can be another powerful way of offering the gift of time and attention and care to someone you're beginning to befriend.

Eventually, as a spiritual friendship grows, you will want to use the word "discipleship" as it takes the relationship to another level and introduces a more intentional focus to your conversations. It also gives you permission to stretch and challenge your disciple in a positive, encouraging way.

Every relationship is different, just like with your children. The principles of parenting or discipling stay the same, but the applications take a unique shape with each person. That's why discipleship isn't a "program"; it's a relationship. Every time people try to systematize the discipling process, it runs the danger of becoming mechanical and undermining the relationship that is at the heart of transformation.

FINDING YOUR FIRST DISCIPLE

Jesus channeled His best time and attention into a small cluster of personal relationships. Remember Him frequently asking those telling questions, *What were you talking about? What do you think about this?* Questions were His tool of choice, and transformational relationships and dynamic spiritual growth were the result.

So where will you start?

As you read this book and strengthen your own spiritual foundations, be actively on the lookout for someone you can come alongside. Let's position ourselves for the explosive potential of disciples-making-disciples right here at the starting line.

- Here's the person I want to ask to be my first / next disciple: _____.

- Here is the environment of work / play / hobby / interest where I will be attentive to those who are in need or hungry for connection: _____.

- Here's a young believer in my church who needs mentoring for growth: _____.

- Here's my specific action step: _____.

- Here's the date I will target for starting: _____.

It's usually the deep personal relationships that are missing in today's church in the midst of scores of activities and programs. The objective is to personally engage people and spend time with them, helping them by active listening, proactive encouraging, and transparent sharing. Most church members will say, "I've never been asked these questions in all my years." Let's change that! Together. By seeking opportunities to *do life with.*

DISCUSSION QUESTIONS

1. What feelings get stirred up in you by reading this perspective on discipleship?

2. How would you answer Question #1 right now: *What is the state of your soul?*

3. What would it feel like to ask these four questions to a friend or disciple?

TWO

Seeing the Big Picture
Living the Kingdom Life

It was my first cross-country flight in pilot training, and I was gone for the weekend. Nan was lonely and did something rather out of character. She picked up a Bible and flopped it open to Matthew 10:37, "He who loves father or mother more than Me is not worthy of Me; and he who loves son or daughter more than Me is not worthy of Me." She was devastated. *I do love my father, my mother, and my husband more than You. Maybe I'm not one of Yours!* In the opening of this book, I hinted at a divine ambush that swept Nan and me into the kingdom. Here's the rest of the story.

I came home from that flight just thinking of a cold beer, only to find Nan overflowing with questions, questions, and more questions. Eventually, her quest got to me and became a nameless angst, a pervasive emptiness in our souls that left us hungry and searching for truth: *Why are we here? What is our purpose? If there is a God, how can we know Him?* So the search was on.

We had both grown up in church, but for us it had been merely social and had long since lost its appeal. Yes, the search was on, but for what? We didn't know. *Is there a God or not?* Either it's real or it isn't. I asked my fellow pilots what they believed. Nan had a Baptist friend who talked with her. We read books. We listened to the Mormons. We invited a Presbyterian pastor and his wife over for dinner. Eventually, we joined the First Methodist Church in Big Spring, Texas.

I remember writing on the service bulletin one day, "What is the Holy Spirit?" Later I asked the pastor that question; his answer was, "Just that good feeling you get in church on Sunday." Not helpful. Hungry for something more, we began to tithe and got re-baptized ...but nothing. Nothing changed inside.

After pilot training we were stationed in Sacramento, California for my first assignment. Immediately I joined a gym, and as it so happened, the manager had just been saved. Gary and I began talking and sharing books…and every Sunday Nan and I tried a new church.

Gary gave me the book *They Speak In Other Tongues* by John and Elizabeth Sherrill, which we devoured. *This is what we need!* We just knew that this was real. Then Gary told us of a church in a nearby community whose pastor spoke in tongues. So on a Friday afternoon I called that church, and the pastor told me they were having a meeting that night and asked us to come.

Caught off guard, I told him we had no babysitter. Besides, I had been thinking about a cowboy movie and that cold beer! I told him we would see him on Sunday. I hung up, turned around, took two steps, and stopped. A totally unfamiliar, supernatural compulsion came upon me with unwavering certainty: *Drop everything. Now. And go.*

I told Nan, "Forget dinner. We're going." I called a babysitter who agreed to take our four-month-old son on the spot. Nan gathered everything and off we roared! Only to be lost for over an hour.

"Damn! Where is that blasted church?" We had been driving forever and were hopelessly lost. I was hungry, tired, and growing more irritable by the minute. Cussing isn't exactly the best way to prepare for a service, but it was a habit I hadn't been able to break. The more we drove in circles, the angrier I became. Nan wanted to just stop and eat, but I was determined to find the place. Mercifully, the church finally appeared, and I drug myself grimly to the door about an hour late.

Stepping across the threshold, I was struck almost tangibly by a wave of Presence. Although I didn't have a name for it at the time, it felt like an Alice in Wonderland moment! Foreign. Fantastic. Slightly intimidating but strangely enticing. We entered the meeting as in a dream and felt transformed by the atmosphere. In fact, I never cursed again after that night.

After the meeting concluded, three lieutenants and their wives along with the pastor stayed to talk with us. One by one, they shared their stories of transformation as we sat there on the choir loft floor. Bibles were opened and the scriptures came to life like never before.

My physical hunger was replaced by a spiritual appetite that welled up until it exploded: "Let's do it!" I cried. "I want it now."

Patiently our new friends led us through our "sin history" to repent and believe in Christ, and after discussing Acts 2:39 we wanted to receive the Holy Spirit. We had never experienced the laying on of hands before, much less praying in tongues. An hour later I experienced what I can only describe as an intensely personal experience with God the Father and was given a deep assurance of Him being in charge and my being safe. It is as real to me today as it was that night. And although we didn't know what to call it, it ushered us into the kingdom of God.

The next few weeks were a happy blur. When I wasn't flying, I would follow Nan around the house reading the Bible out loud saying, "Listen to this!" And I'd read some amazing passage from Acts! I lost nearly 15 pounds during those weeks; we were so excited that food became secondary. All we knew was that we could feel God's love and presence. Prayer became life-giving, and we were getting answers to prayer. Everything was new. We were experiencing the kingdom, but it would be some time before we were taught about it.

MORE THAN SALVATION

So let's talk about the kingdom. Americans know quite a bit about church and virtually nothing about the kingdom of God. The term *gospel* is familiar, but few know that the full terminology Jesus used is "the gospel of the kingdom" (Matthew 9:35; Luke 16:16). We abbreviate terms all the time in our vernacular. Wireless networks are "WiFi." The United States of America is just "America" or "the States." And when scripture speaks of the "gospel," it's an abbreviation for a fuller reference to God's kingdom.

In those first weeks and months of following Jesus, we had never heard the word "kingdom," but we kept saying, "We have discovered a world within a world." It's like doing life with Father. It's the realm of His presence, His Spirit. Technically it's the spiritual dimension of being under His authority.

It was this realm that Jesus opened up so that people could experience God, taste His goodness, and feel His power. It's the place where Satan has been stripped of his power, where healings flow. No wonder crowds flocked to hear tell of this marvelous kingdom realm, which He demonstrated by healing every kind of disease (Matthew 4:23). I think of it as the land of restoration.

Listen to the theologian George Ladd as he tries to help us relate to the whole idea of a kingdom.

> In the year 40 BC political conditions in Palestine had become chaotic. The Romans had subdued the country in 63 BC, but stability had been slow in coming. Herod the Great finally went to Rome, obtained from the Roman Senate the kingdom, and was declared to be king. He literally went into a far country to receive a kingship, the authority to be king in Judaea over the Jews. It may well be that our Lord had this incident in mind in His parable (Luke 19:11-27). The kingdom of God is His king-ship, His rule, His authority. (*The Gospel of The Kingdom*, George Eldon Ladd, p. 21)

A MATTER OF AUTHORITY

In Jesus' day, a king had the power of life and death. His authority in his realm was absolute, no questions asked. For us today this level of authority is a little surreal. Ancient history. So how might we grasp the concept of authority in our world?

We love detective stories, so let's go there. We're familiar with the who-done-it, the murderer—he's broken the law, been arrested, and the judge has the authority to sentence the bad guy to a lifetime in prison. But the story doesn't end there because life goes on, just in prison. It's certainly not a pleasant life, but it is a life.

The very first human, Adam, broke the most important law of all when he severed his relationship with God by rejecting His authority. This cost him dearly...and all who followed, and as a result, he was sentenced to live in a world under a sinister, malevolent authority: the devil.

The one who wields this oppressive authority is called "the god of this world," and in this world, just as in a prison, the inmates do a lot of his dirty work for him. As it turns out, all of us live under some form of spiritual authority. Although it's unseen, we feel its effects in serious ways, which is why Jesus introduced His authority, His kingdom, as coming "to proclaim release to the captives, to set free those who are oppressed" (Luke 4:18). Otherwise known as *good news*.

Matthew quotes Isaiah when he describes mankind: "The people who were sitting in darkness saw a great Light, and those who were sitting in the land and shadow of death, upon them a Light dawned" (Matthew 4:16). Yes, he uses poetic language, but when we sum up repetitive human history—our wars, disease, hate, and death—we find words like "darkness" and "the shadow of death" pretty realistic.

Then comes the David and Goliath story of all time: Immanuel comes! God the Son arrives and reverses Adam's rebellion against the purest, most loving authority ever. I love how the angel said, "You shall call His name Jesus, because He will save His people from their sins" (Matthew 1:21). Scripture later describes Jesus as "the last Adam," referring to His bringing us back under God's authority. I imagine it as Jesus cutting off Goliath's head and holding it up before the stunned, cheering crowd of humanity!

The battle for our release took place during Jesus' 40 days in the desert. Here He took the initiative to strip Satan of his authority: "Go, Satan! For it is written, 'You shall worship the Lord your God, and serve Him only'" (Matthew 4:10). The original Adam left the Father's authority only to wind up under Satan's rule. Jesus, the last Adam, remained under Father's authority and won the right to set us free.

Later Jesus explained His authority over Satan in very practical terms. "But if I cast out demons by the Spirit of God, then the kingdom of God has come upon you. Or how can anyone enter the strong man's house and carry off his property, unless he first binds the strong man? And then he will plunder his house" (Matthew 12:28-29). With Jesus the plunder began.

Luke traces Jesus' return to Galilee in the power of the Spirit, standing in His hometown synagogue, and with new authority declaring, "The Spirit of the Lord is upon Me, because He anointed Me to preach the gospel to the poor. He has sent Me to proclaim release to the captives, and recovery of sight to the blind, to set free those who are oppressed, to proclaim the favorable year of the Lord" (Luke 4:18-19). As the enemy's authority is broken in our lives, these are the very freedoms we begin to experience!

NOW AND NOT YET

The American church generally presents Jesus as earning and offering individual salvation, which is true. But often the impact of His kingdom breaking into our world system is missed. Jesus definitely has come to set us free from our sin consequences: guilt, Satan, and death...but He did much more. Jesus inaugurated a kingdom that operates in a power only partially now revealed, a power that will eventually come full blown and ultimately replace Satan's grip on the earth! To speak theologically, the kingdom is both present and future. Now and not yet. His parables speak of the kingdom as a mustard seed and as leaven—something whose potency is revealed gradually over time (Matthew 13:31-33).

Matthew sums up Jesus' preaching as, "Repent, for the kingdom of heaven [or kingdom of God] is at hand" (Matthew 4:17). John the Baptist had already begun to prepare people for Jesus by convincing them that they needed to undergo a radical change that required more than simply being a Jew. So many were poised to hear about a new King and a new realm, and as He taught about "the gospel of the kingdom," people were healed from diseases and demonic oppression. Crowds came and followed Him in awe. They were quick to point out that Jesus taught with an authority completely unlike their other teachers. Indeed, this was an issue of authority...and Jesus demonstrated it.

This authority shift created quite a stir. Questions and rumors were flying furiously. *What is this kingdom that Jesus is talking about? What does He mean that His kingdom is at hand? What's it like? How is it different from other kingdoms we've seen?* They must have asked these questions because Jesus answered them!

First He both announced and demonstrated the authority of His kingdom. Then He began explaining how very different it was to live in this kingdom. Imagine listening to Jesus teach the Sermon on the Mount (Matthew 5-7), watching the faces of those hearing these life-changing truths for the first time. It was radical then, and it's radical now. Only a few years ago, a significant portion of the American church considered these descriptions of kingdom life so transcendent that they were surely about the future, when Christ will return! But no, these elements of kingdom life are meant for today.

Jesus' kingdom has a King, a King who is God Himself. But this King is not some remote source of power; He is intimate and accessible. He is our "Father." In fact the goal of living under Father's authority is "so that you may be sons of your Father who is in heaven" (Matthew 5:45). "Your Father knows what you need before you ask Him," Jesus affirms, *so here's how you can pray and what you can expect* (Matthew 6:8-13). When you pray this way, you "seek first His kingdom and His righteousness, and all these things [food, clothing, provisions] will be added to you" (Matthew 6:32-33).

In fairy tales the prince marries the princess, and they live happily ever after. Yet our experience in life tracks another, less-happy story line: sexual abuse, divorce, adulteries, suicides, mental illness, dysfunctional families, addictions, sex trafficking. In light of this Jesus is very realistic in describing what is important in His kingdom and how it will bring us into conflict with the culture around us.

THE VALUES OF THE KINGDOM

His starting point in the Sermon on the Mount is a list of values both counter-cultural and counter-intuitive, all anchored in humility. Then He recommends an unexpected strategy: using your hurts to experience Father's comfort. Jesus says that His kingdom prioritizes meekness—the quality of being easy to lead. His next virtue is not the American dream but the very opposite of materialism: to hunger and thirst for righteousness. Oh, and He loves those who extend mercy in a broken world. Then He calls us to imagine a world in which people desire purity of heart and become peacemakers (Matthew 5:3-9).

37

It was not by accident that Jesus anticipated what would happen next, for He capped off this list (the Beatitudes) with a backhanded warning. "Blessed are you [who live this way] when people insult you, persecute you, and falsely accuse you, because of [your relationship to] Me" (Matthew 5:11). Jesus understood the cost of living the kingdom life in a sin-sick culture.

This is not at all the "come to Jesus, and all your problems will be solved" message popular in some circles. It is a radical call to follow Jesus in a committed, all-out loyalty to another realm. The result: those who enter this realm will become like salt, which against all odds attracts people and acts as a preserving influence upon societies. In fact, Jesus was already foreseeing those who would follow Him and become "the light of the world," the church (Matthew 5:13-14). He envisioned a people who would model a new way to live.

It may not be obvious to today's Christians that Jesus never described His people by the now familiar term of *Christian*. Rather He called His followers "disciples of the kingdom" (Matthew 13:52), badging them as representatives of a new order, a new set of values, a new authority.

REDISCOVERING FATHER

The problem is that we don't yet understand the true character of Father God. Instinctively, we assume Him to be demanding and severe. And we couldn't be more wrong. Who did Jesus invite to follow Him and enter the kingdom? Sinners.

"A man had two sons," Jesus begins the famous prodigal story in Luke 15:11-32. The ungrateful, arrogant younger boy hates his father and demands his inheritance. He can't wait to get as far away as possible. Be on his own. Run his own life. Every dad listening to Jesus was hooked by the outrageous injustice of it. It made their blood boil just hearing it. Even when this sorry, no-good son returns, his view of his father has not changed. He doesn't love his father any more than before; he just has no other place to go.

All the money wasted! All the shame he brought on his father! You have to wonder: at what point in the story did this crowd begin to feel the shock wave of Jesus' description of God, describing what no Jewish father would ever tolerate or forgive? This mistreated father isn't nursing his hurt or taking revenge; instead, he's longing for his son! He hurts for his son. Waits with vigilance for his return. And when at last he glimpses his dirty boy trudging up the road, he flies to him with outstretched arms, embracing, weeping, and kissing.

I'll bet Jesus was smiling as he watched the confusion on the faces of His listeners. Then He reaches in deeper. The father brings out his best robe, his signet ring, a party. It's unfathomable in the extreme. This is a God they have never known.

The father Jesus paints loves the undeserving. And while that was slowly sinking in, He went for the kill, introducing the older, hard-working son. The good son, the one who stayed and worked dutifully, turned on his father in protest at the lavish reception of his deadbeat brother. As Jesus holds up a mirror for His listeners, you can almost hear a pin drop. They are expecting the older brother to be the hero of the story; instead, he misunderstands his father as severely as the younger. Jesus' depiction of Father is met with a palpable silence.

This kingdom has a King, and the King is our Father. The one in Jesus' story is none other than the God they have heard of all their lives but never known. The robe, the ring, the party—it's all there in the kingdom!

ENTERING THE KINGDOM

Our personal return to the Father was equally challenging. Nan and I struggled as we felt our way along a most unfamiliar road, searching for what we sensed but couldn't see. *Where's our road to the Father? How can we find what our hearts long for?*

Looking back, I know we would say that the Father's love for us felt radical. It was when Nan first read Jesus' demand for ultimate commitment that she realized she was not yet "in" but "out." Really it could be no other way. You have to experience the "out" in order to enter the "in." Read His words again, just like you did the first time...

Confess Me before men, and I will confess you before the Father. Deny Me before men, and I will deny you before My Father. I did not come to bring peace but a sword. Loyalty to Me will divide families. If you love anyone more than Me, you cannot enter. You are to take up your cross and follow Me. But this I promise, he who has found his life will lose it, and he who has lost his life for My sake will find it. (Matthew 10:32-39, my translation)

Jesus kept His word to us. The night we surrendered to Him, we felt so radically loved that loving Him above all others seemed perfectly natural. This type of faith was new to us. We had a vague belief in Jesus before, but our new friends helped us personally come to Him and confess our sins. He accepted us, forgave us, cleansed us, and filled us with Himself. We were overwhelmed and deeply changed, much to the consternation of our family and friends.

Then we understood why Jesus told a Pharisee who was searching for the kingdom that he needed to be re-birthed spiritually in order to see God's kingdom. It made sense. The realm in which Father's love and power is experienced is spiritual, so only His Spirit can recreate our inner being so that we belong there (John 3:3). We couldn't learn enough fast enough!

Nan and I had never heard about the kingdom, the supernatural part, the real part. This is what we were looking for all along, but we didn't have the vocabulary. Suddenly we felt like we were standing beside Peter when Jesus said to him, "Flesh and blood did not reveal this [My real identity] to you, but My Father who is in heaven." And if I may paraphrase His next words: "I also say to you Peter that upon this revelation of Who I am, I will build My church; and the gates of Hades will not overpower it. I will give you the keys of the kingdom" (Matthew 16:17-18).

For the first time ever, we experienced being the church and representing the kingdom. We also began to understand why Jesus said, "People don't put new wine into old wineskins or they'll burst, but new wine requires new wineskins" (Matthew 9:17). This new wine of the Holy Spirit was full of power, and we suddenly felt like we were part of the church in the book of Acts. All over America the Spirit was transforming people from traditional churches, requiring many to leave and form new churches, communities that could accommodate the intense fervor of faith, prayer, worship, miracles, and passion needed to change the world.

Jesus brought His disciples into the kingdom and prepared them to launch His church by "taking what is His [authority over the devil] and revealing it to us [the church]" (John 16:14). And His kingdom disciples now are proving to be the very "salt" and "light" He spoke about at the beginning of His ministry. He is even in our day turning the world upside down.

Through the Holy Spirit, men and women in ethnic groups all over the world are being adopted into Jesus' band of brothers to whom He said, "All authority has been given to Me in heaven and on earth. Go therefore and make disciples of all the ethnic groups, baptizing them in the name of the Father and the Son and the Holy Spirit, teaching them to observe all that I commanded you; and lo, I am with you always, even to the end of the age" (Matthew 28:18-20).

We are His radically-loved disciples today. We are the ones who "seek first His kingdom and His righteousness" every day. This is our identity, our purpose, and our joy. We are His people, the fruit of His resurrection. Welcome to doing life with!

Now let's talk about church.

DISCUSSION QUESTIONS

1. Before you read this chapter, what did "the kingdom of God" mean to you? How has this reading changed your view?

2. How is being in the kingdom different than being in a church?

3. When you hear that God is the King of the kingdom and wants to have all authority in your life, how does that make you feel?

4. How do we "lose our lives" so that we can find them?

THREE

Unrolling the Blueprint
Jesus' Design for His Church

"If you get where you are going, where will you be?"

I sat frozen like a deer in headlights. Nan and I were attending First Methodist Church that Sunday morning when the pastor leaned over the pulpit and launched that question directly into my chest where it exploded quietly. A seed was planted.

I don't think I heard any more of that sermon, but a fuse had been lit. I'm usually a "present tense" kind of guy, living in the moment without a whole lot of thought for the future. I had never asked myself where I was going. I was just going! But the pastor's question became a game-changer, a come-to-Jesus moment.

I said to myself, *Okay, I'm promoting myself to general in my imagination. How does that feel? Hmm. Doesn't feel much different from being a lieutenant...except maybe I drive a Cadillac instead of a Chevrolet.* I can't explain it, but somehow in that brief moment I knew my future was not in the Air Force. But where was it? *Why am I here? What is my purpose?*

Fast forward to my first duty station flying out of McClellan Air Force base just outside Sacramento. This is where I came to Christ, encountered the Holy Spirit, and eight days later was called by God to preach the gospel. The quest had led me to Jesus and to a dynamic of fellowship, worship, and the supernatural gifts of the Spirit beyond my wildest dreams. But unknown to me at that time, I lacked God's plan, what we call vision: an internal picture of a future that God intends to fulfill. That was next on God's agenda.

Soon we began to get a steady stream of traveling evangelists, prophets, and teachers coming out of a church in Waco, Texas to our little band of believers with a message that rocked my world: Everything we see in the early church is for today! Apostles, prophets, elders, Holy Spirit power, miracles, every believer a priest, church planting, city transformation—it's all being restored by God.

So that's what we began to expect church to be. The book of Acts became a blueprint for what we were building there in California. And what's sweet is that it was happening! People were coming to Christ. They were getting healed and delivered. Some of the signs and wonders we read about on Bible pages were showing up in our community too. We were electrified by it...and continue to be to this day.

The modern church in America is doing many things well. It has largely unshackled itself from the fossilization of outdated, irrelevant modes of ministry to become highly pragmatic in speaking the language and culture of the contemporary world. But in this progression, the point of reference for what church is, at its essence, rarely begins with the early church. Rather than try to undo recent progress in church strategies, let's marry the best of Acts with the best of contemporary thought so that both are honored and neither is compromised.

And even though most people are not church-planters, it's useful to get a quick overview of how the early church fell into disrepair and how God has been restoring those foundations across the ages. This gives us a sense of context, of where we fit in God's larger plan as we seek to do church well in our own day.

The early church that turned the Roman world upside down—this church was diluted and deconstructed into a corrupt, institutional shell of its original power only a couple hundred years later. Once Constantine became the first Roman emperor to convert to Christianity, the church that had prospered powerfully under persecution quickly fell apart as the state coopted it in the Edict of Milan (in AD 313). The church became a rising star politically with the result that the ranks swelled with unconverted "Christians." State and church joined at the hip, compromising the gospel and allowing society to slowly sink into what would later be called the Dark Ages.

If you step back and look across the mountaintops of revival history, you will begin to see a pattern. It looks as if God's Spirit is restoring the doctrines and practices of the early church, one revival and one movement at a time. The most famous was Martin Luther's Ninety-Five Theses in 1517 resulting in the restoring of the bedrock truths of justification by faith and *sola scriptura* ("scripture alone"). About the same time, William Tyndale published the Bible in English for the first time, based upon translations directly from the Hebrew and Greek.

John Calvin first wrote his *Institutes of the Christian Religion* in 1536, sparking a return to Augustinian theology through Switzerland, parts of Germany, England, Scotland, France, and the Netherlands. John Wesley birthed an apostolic movement across Great Britain by recovering church-planting with lay leadership and personal discipleship during his long and productive life, spanning from his conversion in 1738 to his death in 1791.

A powerful visitation of the Holy Spirit transformed the Moravians in 1727, resulting in the first mass Protestant missionary movement. The First Great Awakening swept the colonies during the 1730's and 1740's under the preaching of Jonathan Edwards and George Whitefield, while the Second Great Awakening followed between 1790 and 1800. A prayer revival started in New York City in 1858 led by Jeremy Lanphier that reached its height with 10,000 people per day gathering for sustained prayer; other cities followed.

The revivals that took place in Topeka, Kansas under Charles Fox Parham in 1901 were characterized by experiences with the Holy Spirit accompanied with speaking in tongues and a strong emphasis upon divine healing. An associate of Parham, William Seymour, was used by God to lead the Azusa Street Revival in 1906, which would become the birthplace of the Pentecostal movement.

In 1947 there was a move of the Spirit in Waco, Texas that emphasized a return to the pattern of church life seen in the book of Acts. "Dad" Ewing had been a Presbyterian elder who experienced the filling of the Holy Spirit accompanied with tongues and prophesy. Influenced by an apostle from England, he and his team came to realize that God was sovereignly restoring the church to the purity and power seen in the early church. They had daily Bible studies that led them to believe in the relevance of modern day apostles and prophets, as well as all the supernatural gifts of the Holy Spirit. Teachers, evangelists, and church planters flowed from Waco, spreading what was called the "New Testament Church Vision" to many nations.

The Apostle Paul declared that Jesus would "present to Himself the church in all her glory, having no spot or wrinkle or any such thing; but that she would be holy and blameless" (Ephesians 5:27). This promise causes us to look back over church history amazed at all that the Holy Spirit has accomplished; it also inspires us to look forward to each fresh new move of the Spirit that propels us toward this glorious finish!

PICKING UP THE BATON

The more we came to understand of God's heart for His church and where we stood in the flow of history, the more we felt like we *were* the New Testament Church! We were picking up the baton from those who had come before, taking the next step toward the model of Acts. We could identify with those first Christians who came out of a dead religious system into the breath-taking atmosphere of the supernatural, fueled and led by the Holy Spirit.

We were starting over. "No more man-made religion" was our heart cry! No more denominational hierarchy, formality, or liturgy. Yes, we sometimes threw out the baby with the bath water, but they were what I call good mistakes (doing the wrong things for the right reason).

God was in our midst. We were absorbed with Him. Worship was passionate and sincere. We couldn't get enough. It was almost like we were having to make up for all the wasted years. Every gathering was marked by people's stories: answers to prayer, divine appointments, miracles. Some were pretty crazy like, "I ran out of gas and had no money, so I prayed and God filled my tank and I drove home." Or, "My roof was leaking, and I prayed about it and God fixed the leak."

I remember when one of our two dogs was killed, the remaining dog grieved severely until we laid hands on her and prayed the prayer of faith in Jesus' name. Immediately she stopped grieving and returned to her happy self. When I wasn't flying, I would follow Nan around the house reading about the early church and shouting, "Honey, look at this! You won't believe what God did!" We had our manual for doing church, and it was *The Acts of the Holy Spirit*, penned by Luke.

RECLAIMING THE BLUEPRINT

Jesus knew what He was producing: He was always planning to be "the firstborn among many brethren" (Romans 8:29)—in other words, the prototype for us as the children of God. The model and example of our lives. Having paid for our sins by His death and having conquered death by His resurrection, He breathed the Holy Spirit into His disciples (John 20:22), commissioned them (Matthew 28:18-20), and walked them toward being baptized by the Holy Spirit (Acts1:5,8; 2:1f.) in a way that duplicated and multiplied Himself like no human ever anticipated.

His visible ascension signified that He intended to lead His church from heaven via the Holy Spirit. He would be the real Head, the real headquarters, the home office of the church, which is "His body." And it is this supernatural church that shockingly turned the Roman Empire upside down.

God is vested in blueprints. He took Moses up on a mountain and showed him a pattern for the tabernacle (Exodus 25:9) and commanded him to follow the pattern exactly. He wasn't looking for human ingenuity but rather for a replication on earth of something that had its origins in heaven. It is my belief that the church we see in Acts serves as our pattern for following the Spirit and establishing Christ's rule in His church today.

New Wineskins. Jesus' first miracle was turning six huge jars full of water into wine; everyone said this new wine was the best they had ever tasted (John 2). Later He elaborated on this picture to explain why the Jewish system would not be able to contain His new wine, the Holy Spirit. The powerful force of new fermentation would burst an old wineskin that had grown hard and brittle—the Mosaic Law (Matthew 9:17). The purpose of His church would be to merely contain the dynamic of the Holy Spirit in the lives of His people.

Historically, denominations that were birthed out of Holy Spirit revival become less and less friendly to the life-giving dynamic of the

Holy Spirit over time. And the Spirit does not like to be managed or constrained by human structures. Jesus' parable of the wineskins teaches us that the first rule of church life is to maintain a friendly environment for the Holy Spirit. Tradition in any culture tends to say, "The old wine is better" while every generation needs encounters with the Holy Spirit that are producing new forms of life-giving churches. New life, yet directed by the original pattern.

THE FIVE-FOLD LEADERSHIP GIFTS

Nothing happens without leadership.

Suppose we wanted to reach Muslims in an area of the world; what might we do? Well, we could circulate a paper informing people of the need, hold a conference, and then hear proposals? Or, we could just watch as the first missionary movement is birthed in Antioch (described in Acts 13:2-4) and go to school on how they did it. When we look at that passage, the first thing we notice is that the Holy Spirit moves two men into apostolic ministries. Now connect the dots: the attention given to the Holy Spirit and the multiplication of apostles to lead the charge.

Apostles. New wineskin leadership begins with apostles—men anointed to generate bold, new initiatives to plant churches, train leaders, and transform regions. There is a reason Jesus trained men as apostles before birthing the church; Paul made it clear in 1 Corinthians 12:28 that it is this ministry that needs to be at the forefront of church planting endeavors: "God has appointed in the church, first apostles, second prophets, third teachers...."

Paul seems to associate Jesus' ascension into heaven with His distribution of personal anointing into five different ministries: apostles, prophets, evangelists, pastors, and teachers (Ephesians 4:10-11). Clearly Jesus operated in all five ministries, but He chose to divvy this package of gifts into five different types of leaders—five avenues to fully equip God's people to expand the kingdom of God.

If I picture the hand of God operating through these five types of leaders, I see the apostle as the thumb because only the thumb touches all the other fingers. Apostles are pioneer builders who recognize the need of churches for the other gift ministries. I think of the apostle as the general contractor who oversees the foundation and framing, then brings in the plumbers and electricians and other subcontractors—in this case prophets, evangelists, pastors, and teachers. There was a reason in the Old Testament that conquering kings cut off the thumbs of their enemies: this loss cripples a person's functionality comprehensively. By denying the ongoing work of modern prophets, old wineskin leadership has cut off the thumbs of the church.

Prophets. To understand the role of New Testament prophets today, let's begin by noticing some acts of Jesus that you may not have associated with the prophet role. Jesus saw Nathanael coming and "read his mail"… by which I mean, He spoke a prophetic insight about Nathanael that caused this man to feel known and understood by God (John 2:47-49). The effect upon this young skeptic was a complete turnaround. And it was the Prophet Jesus who told the woman at the well that she was living with a man who was not her husband in spite of her five previous husbands (John 4:18). That word changed her life and affected the whole city!

There is a difference between prophesying and being "a prophet." Paul seems to think that every believer has the potential for prophesying, and he must be speaking from experience when he talks about prophesying over unbelievers and disclosing some of their secrets (1 Corinthians 14:25). Apparently there were a number of prophets in the Corinthian church, and it was their influence that was being multiplied into others (1 Corinthians 14:29-30).

Yet clearly not everyone is a *prophet*. Prophetic leaders carry an anointing and an authority to speak the "now word of God" so that local churches can better cooperate with what the Spirit is doing in their midst. There were prophets already at Antioch when Barnabas and Saul were set apart in apostolic ministries, so it looks like the prophets set the stage for this powerful turning point in church history (Acts 13:1-4).

There are three other leadership gifts in the five-fold distribution of Ephesians 4—evangelists, pastors, and teachers. Since these gifts are familiar and common within the American church, I won't venture to describe them here. We're all well-acquainted with their operation.

It is the apostles and prophets that we find restored to the church by building according to a New Testament blueprint. So, what else is part of that early church pattern?

Jesus called people to follow Him and those who did He called disciples. Believing but not following isn't an option.

Disciples are those men and women whose hearts and wills belong to Jesus. We are disciples of the kingdom of God, and as we gather in community, we are the church. Our loyalty belongs to Christ. We represent Him where we live, and we steward our resources for His purposes. Because of these things Jesus calls us His "body" and His "priests" (Acts 9:5; 1 Peter 2:9).

The distinguishing characteristic of a disciple is obedience. It's following the prompting of the Spirit. Jesus even said that whoever did the will of God was His brother and sister (Mark 3:23)—a potent insight into what it means to be "a Christian."

DISCUSSION QUESTIONS

1. As you consider the many ways God has revived His church over the centuries, how does that impact your view of God's "blueprint" for His Body?

2. Jesus describes the need for new "wineskins" to hold the new "wine" of revelation; how do you see that taking place today?

3. How does the modern church need the ministry of modern apostles and prophets today?

FOUR

Laying a Solid Foundation
Start with Theology

In my fourth church plant, I began with three wonderful couples, all of whom had been badly hurt and disappointed by former church experiences. To make matters worse, one couple had just lost a child. Two were in serious debt as a result of leaving secure jobs to join a church planter who then betrayed them. My question was, *Where should I begin in order to help these battered folks recover?*

Looking back I can see God's wisdom in this initial assignment because putting lives back together is what we do as leaders and Christ-followers. Of course, it's actually God who does it, but it may surprise you that He begins the healing process by changing our understanding of Himself. Which brings us to theology: words about God.

I didn't need to ponder this dilemma very long. A serious study of salvation theology had introduced me to a whole new understanding of a sovereign God...and thus a more accurate view of myself. It was a powerful experience that felt like I got saved all over again! It's always about going back to the basics, isn't it?

You might well ask, "Didn't you believe God was sovereign before? I mean, after all, you went to seminary." Yes, I did believe God was sovereign, but I had little understanding of how sovereign He was or how His sovereignty had shaped the entire structure of my life. And yes, I knew something of God's grace, but then a whole new wellspring of grace came pouring into my soul. I felt myself coming alive. I felt renewed in His love. Buoyed up in a new confidence flowing from, of all things, a theological shift.

This is why I started teaching theology to my church-plant friends as we navigated their tangle of wounds and came into Father's arms. These great truths of God's grace had revolutionized my life, so I wasn't surprised when they did the same for them. It was like water on parched earth, like the joy I see on Nan's face when her houseplants revive and bloom. I assumed they had been taught these truths and simply needed a refresher, but it proved to be otherwise. Those Friday evenings spent studying and discussing the scriptures behind the doctrines brought major changes in their lives. And as they healed and flourished, a church was born.

No matter where we are on the journey—the newest kid on the block or the veteran follower—it is the great doctrines of the faith that reorient us from our dysfunctional focus on self and humanity to focus on God as the single source of salvation. Probably what most American Christians do not realize is how our culture of humanism has seeped into our understanding of scripture and of God Himself.

Americans are pragmatists…and proud of it. We just want life to work, so when we get a dose of understanding about the gospel and taste the grace of forgiveness, it's easy to just move on. But in addition to being pragmatists, we are also explorers—and the most amazing buried treasure has been right under our noses for a long time. The words "theology" and "doctrine" are not exactly hip today. But even though they're "old speak," you may be surprised at their relevance and potency.

So try this word picture: You are visiting your friend on a scorching summer day when he serves you the most refreshing water you have ever tasted. "Man, where does this come from?" you exclaim. Your host says, "Follow me" and leads you to, of all places, his basement where he excitedly points out a number of pipes. "Here is where this water comes from, and I can show you how to get this in your house." The point is simple: these doctrines are simply the "pipes" of truth through which flow the life of Jesus Christ. They're just the pipes, but they deliver something eternal and transformational. Think of it as God's delivery system.

There's another reason Americans have an aversion to doctrine. Too many of us have heard doctrine taught in some drab, mundane, bland fashion. Ugh. No, no, a thousand times no! Imagine hearing about God's supernatural, life-giving help from someone without joy! We've all had our fill of that, thank you very much. To intellectually know the truth but not taste the life inside it is too awful. Come, let's drink our fill of Father's life-giving grace together.

THE WORLD OF GRACE

Recently I listened to a friend tell stories about living for Christ among his Muslim employees in Malaysia and something hit me afresh. He said, "They don't know about forgiveness or grace. They have no reference point." Realizing that his secretary Sue couldn't grasp the concept of grace, he looked for an opportunity. At the end of the month he handed her the usual list of small bonuses for things people had done well; meanwhile, he quietly slipped ten times as much into her pay envelope. He could see her through the glass wall as she opened it, and her eyes got big.

When she rushed in to ask, "What have I done to deserve this?" his answer was, "Nothing." But she pressed him, "Come on, tell me. I must have done something." "No, absolutely nothing, Sue. I just wanted you to experience grace. You needed the money, but you didn't earn it." What hit me in this story was the need for all of us to have fresh reference points, fresh experiences of undeserved help.

The doctrine of grace takes us by the hand into a world like no other: the Father's world. You might think of these doctrines as a road map leading us to the help we long for. *How much does He love us? How far does His love go? When did He start loving us? Why does He love us?* Now, when you put your own name into these questions and hear the answers, you will see that grace takes us far beyond forgiveness. Far, far beyond.

Christians know the delicious grace of forgiveness, yet in spite of that, many live under daily efforts to measure up. The thing is, grace is counter-intuitive; strangely enough, only grace can overpower sin. And hopefully you're eager for more of it, more of what Paul injects into every letter, "Grace to you" being his constant refrain.

How can grace deliver us from sin? The fact that we have to ask this question means we may be as surprised as Sue when we look into our "pay envelope" (the doctrines). We may discover that while we know a measure of grace first-hand, our understanding may be more limited than we suspect. There is, deep within us, an almost irrevocable desire to measure up, a desire surprisingly accomplished by grace.

One of my little sayings is that we all start out as "prodigals" but eventually recognize ourselves in the older brother. Wow, that's disheartening! But we all have the T-shirts to prove it, don't we? Let's change that.

Where can we find this grace?

TOTAL DEPRAVITY: OUR SIN PROBLEM

I can tell you where grace began seeping into my soul because it came from an unlikely source. You may think me strange, but the doctrine that cracked open my inherited misconceptions of God (and thus me) is called Total Depravity: the understanding that we come into this world with a bias toward self and a commitment to our own self-rule. In other words, we are sinners in both nature and behavior, and we actively resist God's rightful lordship of us.

Believe me, Americans as a whole do not like this doctrine. It undermines the "me, me, me" humanism that perfumes our culture. But it also explains why I can't produce anything good by myself.

Frequently I am asked why this doctrine is so important to me, and the answer is simple. When at last I discovered this truth, I shouted, "I'm normal!" While planting my first church, I kept expecting to be more spiritual, more competent, more capable...and the more I came up short, the more I began to carry some pretty heavy condemnation. Total Depravity explained all that.

Consider this illustration: The closer you get to God, the brighter the light. Every room seems clean in the dark. A 40-watt bulb reveals a few things; 100 watts reveals much more; and 1000 watts unveils more than you would ever want to see! The closer I got to God, the more aware I was of my inability to live up to His wonderful words. I kept expecting to find something good in myself...only to be bitterly disappointed. I would reach into my soul, hoping to find some shred of humility or patience or desire to serve and be devastated to find that I was only getting worse. Maybe you know the feeling of trying so hard to measure up.

The doctrine of Total Depravity collects the many descriptions of man's sinful nature in scripture and summarizes God's analysis of our plight. When Adam declared himself God's enemy by renouncing His right to rule, the consequences went straight into me! Turns out, I'm packing some of Adam in me, even after I "become a Christian!" Yikes. Here is some of what God says about the human condition.

- John 3:19-20, "This is the judgment, that the Light has come into the world, and men loved the darkness rather than the Light." *Sad to say, our wills love the darkness.*

- Romans 3:9,11, "All are under [the power of] sin.... There is none who seeks for God." *God has to seek us first.*

- Romans 8:7, "The mind set on the flesh is hostile toward God; for it does not subject itself to the law of God, for it is not even able to do so."

- Romans 7:21-24, "I find then the principle that evil is present in me, the one who wants to do good. For I joyfully concur with the law of God in the inner man, but I see a different law in the members of my body, waging war against the law of my mind and making me a prisoner of the law of sin which is in my members."

- 2 Corinthians 4:3-4, "If our gospel is veiled, it is veiled to those who are perishing, in whose case the god of this world has blinded the minds of the unbelieving so that they might not see the light of the gospel of the glory of Christ."

It's really not a pretty picture. I remember my mother teaching me that all people are good if you treat them that way, and I grew up believing her "doctrine": a blind faith in people's basic goodness. Even when I became born again and realized I was a sinner, this bedrock remained. I thought I was a "sinner-lite," thus forcing Him to drill down to my flawed, unbiblical belief.

Someone will object: *Aren't we free to choose God? If not, how are we free?* This paradox agitates our western, democratic, equalitarian minds. The problem is that we use the word "free" in two very different ways. We are "free" to love our enemies…but it simply isn't our nature. *Why not?* Well, we don't want to. No one is stopping us from forgiving, from being patient, from loving others more than ourselves. Man is free to choose God in the sense that nothing is stopping him…except himself. We inherited Adam's nature.

We also recognize that people often do good things; some do amazingly heroic acts of kindness or sacrifice. This is certainly true. The real test, however, is to reference a man's "good works" with how they seem to God. Only God is good (Mark 10:18), and man in his natural condition can do nothing out of love for God. What motivates the "good person" is usually an altruism that has its roots in pride or may result from a desire for significance, meaning, or purpose; whatever it is, it is not from or for God. Even after salvation, depravity remains part of our reality and propels toward the gospel of grace.

Remember, we are transitioning from a man-centered worldview to a radically different: God-centered perspective. Which takes us to God's redemption plan!

UNCONDITIONAL ELECTION: GOD CHOOSES US

How does God draw our hearts to respond to His love when our wills are dead set against Him? That's a problem, isn't it? Here's my story.

Me, go on a spiritual retreat at age nineteen? I don't think so. But as a new Air Force Academy cadet, the pressure was unrelenting; I would have done almost anything to go somewhere where no one would be yelling at me. So I was in! While savoring the relaxation, I found that these darn Navigators kept trying to sit beside me on the bus and talk about Jesus. But I was one wary cadet: no one is sitting beside me. Get away.

Fast forward some five years later and witness an amazing change of heart. I wanted God and was looking for Him! Clearly, something mysterious and powerful had occurred in my heart without my permission. God took the initiative silently, behind the scenes, and my desire to know Him was awakened. The dramatic change certainly surprised my friends!

How does one explain this sudden, out-of-the-blue turnaround? The Bible word that addresses this mysterious phenomenon is election. The doctrine is appropriately designated, "Unconditional Election" because God's choice of whom He will call to Himself is not predicated upon anything we do. Wayne Grudem explains the process this way: "Election is an act of God before creation in which He chooses some people to be saved, not on account of any foreseen merit in them, but only because of His sovereign good pleasure" (*Biblical Doctrine*, p. 282).

With Adam's nature passed on to us, we aren't "free" or able to choose God...but He is free to choose us. Why would He set His love upon us? God has revealed at least a piece of this mystery when He says, "He chose us in Him before the foundation of the world... [and] predestined us to adoption as sons through Jesus Christ to Himself, according to His good pleasure" (Ephesians 1:4-5). The only reason He offers is "His good pleasure"; this is God's sovereignty and grace in high gear!

Here are a few additional insights from scripture:

- John 1:13, We "were born [again], not of blood nor of the will of the flesh nor of the will of man, but of God."

- John 15:16, "You did not choose Me but I chose you."

- Acts 13:48, "As many as were ordained to eternal life believed."

Is the Will Free? Martin Luther's famous book, *The Bondage of The Will*, has this quote: "Free will is an empty term because it is precisely man's will that does not want to know God."

At the age of 25, I believed that I had chosen God...in spite of the many Scriptures that plainly say that I was incapable of initiating faith since I was "dead in my trespasses and sins," "under the rule of the prince of the power of the air," and was "a son of disobedience." Oh, I forgot to mention, "a child of wrath" (Eph. 2:1-3). I simply had not at that point in my Christian walk deeply understood my fallen nature. I knew I was a sinner; I knew that I was a saved sinner; but I had only a vague idea of how Adam's nature had affected me personally.

Paul writes to his friends in Thessalonica, "Knowing, brethren beloved by God, His choice [election] of you...." How can Paul be so sure these are God's elect? He continues, "Because our gospel did not come to you in word only, but also in power and in the Holy Spirit and with full conviction" (1 Thessalonians 1:4-5). Obviously many others heard Paul preach without believing, which led Paul to credit God alone with the conversion of those who did repent and believe.

Understanding Faith. Faith is a word that is casually and frequently used by Christian and non-Christian alike...but rarely defined. We use it as a noun, but it carries with it the force of a verb (think "trust"). We have faith in God, whereas sometimes Americans may refer to having faith in something undefined. For example, it's not uncommon to hear, "I just have faith" without the object being specified. It may be a sort of Han Solo type of faith in faith.

The Bible uses the word faith to mean *the ability to recognize who God is so as to honor Him as God.* Those who are God's enemies, those who love sin and hate the Light have no ability whatsoever to recognize and honor God for who He is. Paul makes this painfully clear in his letter to the Ephesians where he seems to shovel layer after layer of man's impossibility to believe (Ephesians 2:1-3) upon humans until he is sure we know that we have "no hope and are [without] God in this world" (Ephesians 2:12).

After burying us thoroughly Paul then explains how God has mercy upon us, makes us alive, and raises us up with Christ, which explains how we wind up having faith. This ability we call faith is the gift of God; it's not from ourselves, and he even states the reason for God working this way: "So that no one may boast." No one can say, "At least I believed," for even belief is a unique gift from God.

The American Value of Fairness. American culture places a strong emphasis on fairness. The appeal to fairness is as ubiquitous as the appeal to free speech. The cry of a young child is often, "It isn't fair!" and this is true. We aren't born with equal anything except our original created value of being made in God's image. We don't have equal advantages in our families, in birth order, time in history, gender, talents, or opportunities. The sage is right, "Life is not fair." Yet somehow we Americans persist in believing that unfairness is just plain wrong.

Fairness and justice are different but blurred in our culture. The fairness doctrine says that whatever benefit you receive I should receive also. It is man-centered. Justice is about receiving what you deserve, and the standard bearer is God. When the two concepts are used interchangeably, as they often are, the casualty is almost always our understanding of justice. We humans instinctively interpret life by comparing man with man, which blinds us to the God-centered reality of justice.

Some, still struggling with the idea of fairness, try to explain God to the western mind by interpreting "foreknow" as God seeing into the future and knowing who would choose to believe. While this view initially seems to present God as being fair, it still leaves Him creating people whom He knows will choose badly. God refuses to be explained when what is appropriate is worship, adoration, and submission.

REGENERATION: AWAKENING THE HUMAN HEART

So if the human heart is depraved and unable to respond to God's kingdom invitation...and if God's choice of us is not conditioned by anything we do but only upon His sovereign intent, then how do we find ourselves able at some point to respond to God as Father?

The ancients called this inner transformation "regeneration." A more modern definition is this: *Regeneration is a secret act of God in which He imparts new spiritual life to us* (*Bible Doctrine*, Wayne Grudem, p. 300). So in regeneration God awakens or activates the human heart so that it is able to respond to God's love for the first time. At this point, God's choice of us is mirrored by our choice for Him. This is the next step in the salvation sequence for experiencing conversion and justification.

JUSTIFICATION: ENTERING INTO THE KINGDOM

Once God's election of us is activated and reorients our hearts toward God instead of away from Him, we then experience what we call conversion and justification—two words that describe our part and God's part of our entry into the kingdom.

Wayne Grudem defines conversion as "our willing response to the gospel call, in which we sincerely repent of sins and place our trust in Christ for salvation" (*Bible Doctrine*, p. 307). Conversion is a bit like an iceberg in that only the smallest part is visible. This is man's part in the salvation process: Paul says "that if you confess with your mouth Jesus as Lord, and believe in your heart that God raised Him from the dead, you will be saved" (Romans 10:9).

We would not necessarily know that the greatest part of an iceberg is below the waterline without the help of science, nor would we understand the invisible work of God that enables a man to repent and believe without the revelation given us in scripture. The Father elects, the Son atones, and the Holy Spirit calls us with the result that a previous "child of wrath" now has a will that is able to recognize his need to repent to God and to believe in Jesus.

We share the good news about the kingdom of God, and we rightly tell people that in order to be saved from the wrath of God, they must repent and believe. Those who respond, like Lydia (Acts 16:14), do so because of God's unseen help, but the dramatic change we observe is labeled conversion. It is at conversion that a person actually experiences the forgiveness and acceptance of God.

Coming into God's kingdom through conversion is like entering another world. We experience peace with God at a level we never knew existed; this is the result of God justifying us. "Therefore, having been justified by faith, we have peace with God through our Lord Jesus Christ" (Romans 5:1).

Some have cleverly but mistakenly defined justification as "just-as-if-I'd-never-sinned," but this would only take us back to Adam's sinless status in the garden. God does forgive us for our sin and lifts the consequences of that sin, but He goes much farther than that. He also declares us to be righteous—a status that Adam never earned.

Grudem's definition is this: "Justification is an instantaneous legal act of God in which he (1) thinks of our sins as forgiven and Christ's righteousness as belonging to us, and (2) declares us to be righteous in his sight" (p. 316). Justification is God's response to our act of conversion...which in itself is our response to God's original act of election.

Justification by faith alone is a cornerstone doctrine—one for which Martin Luther famously interceded in the Protestant Reformation of 1517. God fulfilled justice by punishing Jesus for our sins. Biblically, He propitiated (satisfied) His wrath and atoned for our sins.

Paul knew how important it was for the welfare of the Roman church to really understand how God could justify undeserving sinners, so he explained it in chapter 3. "All have sinned and fall short of the glory of God, being justified as a gift by His grace through the redemption which is in Christ Jesus; whom God displayed publicly as propitiation in His blood through faith. This was to demonstrate His righteousness, because in the forbearance of God He passed over the sins previously committed; for the demonstration, I say of His righteousness at the present time, so that He would be just and the justifier of the one who has faith in Jesus" (Romans 3:24-26).

Confusion about this truth always brings legalism, condemnation, and loss of peace....while clarity about this truth brings a confidence and security like none other. We have talked about the father's passionate embrace of the returning prodigal. Not only does he forgive the wayward son, but he lavishes him with kisses, with his best robe, his ring of authority, and his shoes. Not to mention the party! This covering is a picture of forgiveness...but more than that: it symbolizes His approval, acceptance, and status. All undeserved, all unearned. No wonder Martin Luther was excited.

It's true that justification doesn't change a man's character instantaneously, but the conversion-justification experience does produce a profound change in a person's life. My advice to the prodigal is, *Wear the robe. Enjoy your father. Stay in the party.* Here's how we do that.

SANCTIFICATION: GROWING TO BE LIKE CHRIST

There is an old question that goes like this, *How far did man fall when he sinned?* The answer, *You'll never know until you try to go back.* The great thing is this: it is God who initiates our desire to know Him, to be like His Son, and to be free from sin. He begins the journey back by bringing the gospel to us, giving us a new heart so that we are able to repent and believe. The result is that even in these early stages of our faith walk we experience some pretty profound changes, which we call the beginning of sanctification.

The Bible boldly addresses us as "saints," which means that as followers of Christ, our lives belong to Him and are set apart for Him. I love this, that God honors us with such a high calling and destiny. He also knows that we are a work in progress. Grudem defines the process this way: "Sanctification is a progressive work of God and man that makes us more and more free from sin and like Christ in our actual lives" (p. 326).

As "new creatures" in Christ, our wills are now free to draw near to God, to fellowship with Jesus, and to live in the power of His resurrection life. This is why our growth in Christ is an interplay between the Holy Spirit who prompts and us who respond. Or sometimes don't.

The question of how to grow in Christ must address an overarching issue: *How does the gospel that justifies us also provide us with the power to overcome sin?* How can the gospel transform our character? Any Christian who cannot open his Bible and point to verses that answer these two questions is going to be frustrated by his desire to change.

I love Paul's mind. First he lays down the basic theme, that the gospel is the power of God for salvation/deliverance/freedom (Romans 1:16). By chapter 5 he has explained how the gospel justifies us, and from there he proceeds to explain in Romans 6 how our dying with Christ gives us power over sin. Galatians 2:20 crystalizes this truth into a form that has been very effective in helping me identify with Christ at the very point of my need. In fact, this is precisely how we experience the power of the gospel delivering us from particular sins. I call this process "going to the cross." It is an act of faith to recognize our being with Him in His dying for our sins. Personally, I first learned this truth, not in church and not in seminary, but from Roy Hession's book, *Calvary Road.*

The Bible word for Christ's character in us is "righteousness," and Romans 1:17 explains how the gospel actually downloads His humility, patience, purity, wisdom, and all the other virtues of Christ into our lives. "In [the gospel] the righteousness of God is revealed from faith to faith." We can go to the cross in order to be freed from the grip of a particular sin, but that doesn't automatically change our character. What we need is Christ's character—the righteousness of God— revealed and applied to our souls. The Holy Spirit has to make this transaction real, and we have to receive His righteousness by faith.

Forgiveness, check. Power over sin, check. His character made available to us, check. But there is more. "In Him was life" (John 1:4), and He shares that life with us. In John 15, Jesus described Himself as "the vine" that contains the sap (the life); he describes us as the branches, drawing everything we need from Him in order to produce fruit. It's a graphic picture! The question that comes next is, *How?* How can ordinary people whose lives are hectic and filled with so many demands and pressures make this work? The answer: the classic spiritual disciplines, which we will explore in detail in chapter six.

Sanctification requires that we carve out time to cultivate our relationship with Christ. Since we need His life to sustain us every day, it is important to develop the time-honored, biblical ways to meet with Him and experience Him on a daily basis. In addition, our spiritual growth is leveraged through other spiritual practices: biblical study, journaling, being still, listening, fasting, meditation, waiting on God, memorizing Scripture, praying the promises of God, interceding for the needs of others, and worship.

His invitation, "Come to Me, all you who are weary and heavy-laden; and I will give you rest" (Matthew 11:28) is the call to be with Him. His "learn from Me" is a game-changer. The disciplines help you shape your life around Jesus so that your faith can last a lifetime.

PERSEVERANCE OF THE SAINTS: THE SUSTAINING POWER OF OUR FAITH

A troubling question presents itself on this topic: *Can a born-again Christian lose his salvation?* We have all known people who prayed the "sinner's prayer," seemed to love Jesus, but at some point did not follow through and continue their walk of faith. Jesus gave us a definite head's up on this matter when He said, "Not everyone who says to Me, 'Lord, Lord,' will enter the kingdom of heaven, but he who does the will of My Father.... Many will say to Me on that day, 'Lord, Lord', did we not prophesy in Your name...cast out demons...perform many miracles? And then I will declare to them, 'I never knew you; depart from Me, you who practice lawlessness'" (Matthew 7:21-23).

The church has lost its way by defining the Christian as one who is forgiven rather than one who follows. For this reason many are falsely assured they are born again when there is yet no fruit of repentance in their lives. Our proper insistence that we are saved by faith and not by works has too easily become "a faith which produces no works," a belief sanctioned by neither scripture nor Martin Luther.

Into this present-day confusion comes the clear light of doctrine: "The perseverance of the saints means that all those who are truly born again will be kept by God's power and will persevere as Christians until the end of their lives, and that only those who persevere until the end have been truly born again" (Grudem, p. 336).

Jesus also assured us of God's continued grace that would sustain us, His "sheep," throughout our lifetimes. "My sheep hear My voice, and I know them, and they follow Me; and I give eternal life to them, and they will never perish; and no one will snatch them out of My hand" (John 10:27-28). Grudem rightly comments that we are surely included in the "no one" (p. 337), and Jesus intended us to have the confidence that comes from the assurance of our salvation. Fear and insecurity is not to be found in Father's heart.

GLORIFICATION: ENTERING THE NEXT LIFE

Not only will every person chosen by God persevere in faith until heaven, each of us will also be given a resurrection body when we do enter into the full manifestation of His kingdom. Paul was quite eager to undergo this change: "To die is gain," he declared in Philippians 1:21. 2 Corinthians 12:4 says with confidence, "So also is the resurrection of the dead. It is sown a perishable body, it is raised an imperishable body; it is sown in dishonor, it is raised in glory; it is sown in weakness, it is raised in power" (1 Corinthians 15:42-43).

Clearly, God wants us to know that if we have been justified, we shall also be glorified which, no doubt, includes *more* than our bodies but *not less* (Romans 8:30). With the promise of "being like Him when we see Him," as well as having a resurrection body like His, we can identify with Paul's description of groaning, "waiting eagerly for our adoption as sons, the redemption of our body" (Romans 8:23). I think our Father wants to explain enough about who He is, how He works, and what He has in store for us so that we are the most secure, confident, and grateful of all peoples.

And that's really the point of theology—to understand God and ourselves well enough to step into a supernatural relationship with Him. If God's heart is to do life with us (and I think we have established the truth of that), then a solid foundation of theology is what allows us to join Him in intimate, eternal relationship. It is the bridge that connects us and the embrace that holds us throughout our journey in this life and into the next.

DISCUSSION QUESTIONS

1. How do you relate to the idea of doctrine and theology?

2. How real, personal, and consistent is your experience of grace?

3. How do you understand the difference between fairness and justice?

4. Which of these doctrines brings you most joy and life?

FIVE

Grasping the Gospel
Faith and Power in the New Life

It was the spring of 1971. Nan and I were driving back from visiting my brother-in-law Frank and his family in Yakima, Washington. My seminary program was almost complete, and our hearts were full of the "What next?" question. Church-planting was most on our radar; we just wondered where. Maybe Washington state. Maybe Oregon.

The beauty of the northwest was irrefutable, and it didn't seem like too far a stretch from our current home in Sacramento, California. On the drive back, we lingered in some of the communities, driving slowly and observing prayerfully. *God, where do you want us to plant ourselves? Where would you want us to start a church?*

Arriving home around midnight, I reached into the mailbox to retrieve a week-long pile of letters. One envelope bore a postmark from Fayetteville, North Carolina. My breath caught sharply, and I breathed, *You wouldn't!* And yet, even before I opened it, I had an immediate witness of the Spirit.

The letter was from my old friend Tom Looney. Only months before in my hometown of Rocky Mount, North Carolina, I had prayed with Tom for the baptism of the Holy Spirit. A West Point grad, he had just been transferred by his brokerage company to Fayetteville where he reconnected with another classmate, Curry Vaughan. Curry was an army chaplain who was leading a small prayer meeting that had encountered the Holy Spirit in a big way. They wanted to know if I would lead it.

Several months later we were moving our furniture into a rental house in this military town as I began the first church plant of my career. Fresh out of seminary, three small children, and little experience to draw upon—we had a lot to learn, to say the least! And it didn't take long for the mess to hit the fan.

Within four weeks of assuming the pastorship, every single leader in this small group had bailed. Apparently, I wasn't what they had expected, so there Nan and I were with five young believers who wanted to change the world for Jesus. We rolled up our sleeves and got to work, preaching, teaching, counseling, and casting out demons. Yes, demons!

In the early 70s we were all "born-again hippies," just barely on the back side of the Jesus movement, and the local army base seemed like the "wild west" of the spiritual world. Drugs, sex, and rock 'n roll were matched by witchcraft and demonization at every turn, so it was an interesting time and place to cut my teeth as a new church planter.

Meanwhile, I began to experience crippling feelings of inadequacy. I had neither the experience, the coaching, nor the spiritual depth to anchor my soul in the face of such strong spiritual opposition…and it was taking a toll. The sense of not measuring up felt palpable. Looking back on it, I suspect this must have been similar to what Paul experienced church-planting in another "wild west" town where he penned these words. "Wretched man that I am! Who will set me free from the body of this death?" (Romans 7:24).

Providentially, just about this time a friend introduced me to a small, unimpressive looking book—a short biography of the life of Charles Spurgeon—and every page brought a salve to my troubled soul. Spurgeon was a fiery Baptist pastor of New Park Street Church in mid-1800s London, and his passion for God seemed to flow out of a depth of understanding I had never known. The life and message of Spurgeon oozed grace and introduced me to the Father's heart for me at a whole new level.

He loves me! Chose me. Unconditionally. I am really his son, and He is totally for me. This became my ground floor of truth and ushered in a divine joy, an utter relief that has marked all my days since. I read his words hungrily and learned more about how to come immediately to the Father and receive His forgiveness through the blood of His Son.

It was my own spiritual boot camp, and in that crucible I learned how to fight the good fight and lay hold of His life as the source of everything I lacked. The chains of condemnation fell to the side over time as I recognized and applied the power of a glorious gospel.

We all experienced this grace and this gospel when we first came to Christ. It doesn't take long for many of us, though, to adopt the unspoken belief that the rest of the Christian life is up to us. That Christ did His part, and now it's time for us to do ours. We wouldn't say it that way, but our actions betray us—and quickly fail us—as we attempt to live the Christian life without the ongoing power of the gospel engaged. In this chapter we want to explore three elements of gospel power: the blood, the cross, and the resurrection of Christ.

Experience and theology are intended to be soulmates. The fundamental elements of theology that we considered in the last chapter serve as a road map for our journey into experience. Theology organizes Scripture verses into categories thus providing "truth with handles"—otherwise known as doctrines. The Holy Spirit uses doctrine to help bring understanding that stimulates our faith. In this way experience and theology are symbiotic, each feeding the other. That's why I think it will help us to link our experiences of gospel power to the doctrines we're learning about.

THE POWER OF THE BLOOD

We are all experienced lawyers when it comes to justifying ourselves: blaming, excusing, or comparing ourselves with others. So we have some understanding of the word "justify." Self-justification appoints "Self" as judge and jury, but at the end of the day, that pseudo-justification does not work. Shame doesn't give up that easily.

For God Himself to justify you—now that is something indeed! To look deep into our motives, attitudes, words, and deeds as the rightful Judge and declare us forgiven and counted righteous. This is the miracle of the universe.

But a lot had to happen to make this possible. For God to be just He had to have someone innocent take our place and satisfy justice. This He did by sending Jesus to die in our place. His blood, His life for your life and mine!

As we saw in the theology chapter, justification starts with forgiveness and then adds the righteousness we needed but could not produce for ourselves. In an instant of time, Jesus' righteousness became ours! Wow. There is nothing else in the world like it! The cleansing, the freedom from condemnation, the sense of peace. Life-changing. Once experienced, that refreshing sense of inner peace is something you never want to lose. Justified by God Himself: the real thing! This facet of the gospel is "the power of the blood" since John describes how "the blood of Jesus His Son cleanses us from all sin" (1 John 1:7).

Paul seems to have found God's "sweet spot" when he later penned, "and may [I] be found in Him, not having a righteousness of my own derived from the Law, but that which is through faith in Christ, the righteousness which comes from God on the basis of faith" (Philippians 3:9). It is this faith dependence upon Christ alone that satisfies us and glorifies God.

I love that scene in the prodigal story where the father accepts his filthy son and covers his failure and shame by placing his best robe upon him. What a snapshot of justification, demonstrating how thoroughly the son is forgiven by the father while not implying that the son is fully changed inside. By the exchange of Christ's life for our life, the Father counts us righteous. It is the basis upon which He can take us fully into His acceptance. Deeply changing our character so that we are becoming more and more righteous in our thoughts and actions is called sanctification: becoming like Him.

THE POWER OF THE CROSS

Despite the cleaning of guilt and shame in justification, we do still continue to sin. In fact, once we savor the forgiveness, cleansing, acceptance, and love of God, we become much more sensitive to the defiling intrusion of sin. For this reason, we all respond eagerly to the Sunday-by-Sunday invitation to participate in "the power of His blood": "If we confess our sins, He is faithful and just to forgive us our sins, and to cleanse us from all unrighteousness" (1 John 1:9).

Eventually we begin to realize that we are pre-programed to slide back into trying to live up to God's standards by our own will power, so learning to live day-by-day trusting in Christ's righteousness alone is a challenging journey for us all. The apostle Paul gives us hope and advice right at this point as he shares his miserable failures in Romans 7. "The good that I wish, I do not do; but I practice the very evil that I do not wish.... Wretched man that I am!" (7:19,24).

Fortunately, Paul doesn't stop there. He also tells us how he came to live in overcoming power—"Thanks be to God through Jesus Christ our Lord! ....For the law of the Spirit of life in Christ Jesus has set you free from the law of sin and of death" (Romans 7:25, 8:2).

"And may be found in Him, not having a righteousness of my own derived from the Law, but that which is through faith in Christ, the righteousness which comes from God on the basis of faith" (Philippians 3:9). This is the goal!

When Forgiveness Isn't Enough. We all know a "Fred" who has a serious addiction to drugs, alcohol, fits of rage, pornography, gambling (choose one). Or "Sarah" who is bulimic, cuts herself, and is now head-over-heels in credit card debt. Both love Jesus, believe in Jesus, and are faithful members of an excellent church. Sunday by Sunday they crawl into church feeling so awful, so plagued, so despairing. They soak up the forgiveness offered in communion, and hope no one knows what goes on behind the scenes.

When finally Fred and Sarah can take it no longer, they make an appointment with a pastor. The question is this: what will they hear? Will they be lovingly and patiently guided into the power of the gospel to deliver them from a particular habit of sin? Will they be led to experience the power Paul refers to in Romans 6:14, "For sin shall not be master over you, for you are not under law but under grace"?

Fred and Sarah have both read this verse many times and the whole chapter promising the power to break free, and their cry is, "Tell me how? How does this work? How can I experience more than forgiveness?"

Paul is referring to a grace that, like forgiveness, comes from Jesus dying in our place on the cross, but it is experienced differently and often not explained well, if at all. I was not taught this at church or in seminary but thankfully learned the gospel secret to becoming free from the power of a sin habit from Roy Hession in his little book, *The*

Calvary Road. The verse that Hession and the Holy Spirit used to introduce me to this type of power was Galatians 2:20.

Take the first part: "I have been crucified with Christ; and it is no longer I who live, but Christ lives in me." As I began to see myself dying with Jesus, faith came so that I saw it. "I died with Him to that sin. I, Jerry, no longer live, but Christ lives in me." Paul essentially says the same thing in other words in Romans 6:11, "Consider yourselves to be dead to sin, but alive to God in Christ Jesus." But somehow it never became clear to me how to "consider myself" as dying with Him until Galatians 2:20 turned on the lights.

The rest of this verse finishes the transaction: "And the life which I now live in the flesh I live by faith in the Son of God who loved me and gave Himself up on my behalf." Oh to absorb this truth deep inside! Memorize it, meditate on it, and pray these divine truths. The Holy Spirit will release the power of the cross to set you free.

I love it that you don't have to wait until "you calm down" or "get into a better frame of mind." No, once you gain some experience with the power of the cross, you can go there with Him right in the middle of a meltdown or in the middle of a surge of temptation and experience His death bringing you into freedom.

Now you are cooking on the power of the blood and the power of the cross; but there is more power still!

THE POWER OF WEAKNESS

I can imagine someone saying, "The power of weakness... Are you kidding me?" We males do not like being weak; and generally speaking, we go to many lengths to not be weak or to at least cover it up. In fact it would not be unusual to find Christian men praying for God to make them strong because they don't understand God's counter-intuitive way of releasing His strength into a man. Of course God works the same way with women, but I'm more in tune with how men feel about their weaknesses than women. So, allow me to pick on the men.

What if? What if your greatest weaknesses could actually be assets? Instead of being embarrassed about them or trying to hide them, you could use them as a means of receiving God's power in a way that further makes you dependent upon Him.

Paul was in a real predicament. If you have never had "a messenger of Satan" tormenting you (I hope you haven't, but I have), it's horrible. Talk about feeling utterly weak—Paul was there. That's when Jesus came to him and revealed what seems to be a well-kept secret even among Christians.

Listen to Jesus coach Paul, "And He has said to me, 'My grace is sufficient for you, for power is perfected in weakness'" (2 Corinthians 12:9). Jesus promised Paul that His grace would be enough for him based upon a revolutionary principle: *power is released, manifested, comes into fullness in weakness.* When you stop and think about it, that's the way grace always works: desperately needed help that is undeserved.

The tables just got turned on Satan and in such a way that God received all the credit and Paul got all the bennies. How cool is that?

Paul stopped trying to get rid of his weaknesses and needs; instead, he rejoiced over them! He celebrated them. Listen to him right at this point, "Most gladly, therefore, I will rather boast about my weaknesses, so that the power of Christ may dwell in me." Now he goes a step further by declaring, "I am well content with weaknesses, with insults, with distresses, with persecutions, with difficulties, for Christ's sake; for when I am weak, then I am strong" (2 Corinthians 12:9-10).

Translated, this means that rather than be intimidated by inadequacies, you can rest easy (be content) because when you feel unable and insufficient, then you are able to draw God's ability right into the place where you lack it.

This is yet another reason a disciple of Jesus can be comfortable in his or her own skin. We do not live in fear of being "found out," of someone discovering how weak we really are. The amazing thing is that the more we are comfortable with our weaknesses, the more His power can access our hearts and transform us. People around us don't know where the ability comes from; it just shows up. It also marks us with an easy sense of not having to prove ourselves, and this is a most attractive trait. And all this prepares us for the next demonstration of gospel power.

THE POWER OF RESURRECTION

It is incredible to be forgiven for such life-sucking sins as pride, insecurity, impatience, and foolish words; this is the power of the blood. And we have explored the power of the cross to break the compulsions these sins can exert on our souls. Next we watched as Paul's relationship with weakness became his greatest asset. But this still leaves us with a need that the gospel alone can meet. Let's call this the power of resurrection.

Think with me for a moment. Let's say you have recognized a fresh outbreak of pride, and you have tasted the joy of His forgiveness. Perhaps you have visualized your pride being placed on Jesus so that the controlling force of pride was broken. That's a lot of power, but I have a question. How will you produce Christ's character quality of humility to take its place? You know you cannot yourself manufacture humility, nor does forgiveness for pride produce it.

God fully intends to put His resurrection life, His character qualities, into you! This is much more than forgiveness. "He made Him who knew no sin to become sin on our behalf, so that we might become the righteousness of God in Him" (2 Corinthians 5:21). It is His plan to install His character attributes in us, such as wisdom in place of our foolishness...or patience in place of our impatience...or purity in place of our lust. This is no small undertaking. Fortunately, this gospel has the power to transform us over time to become like our Father in His character. The theological word for this process is sanctification, which we began to look at in the last chapter.

I find in myself a great, ongoing need for Christ's righteousness in my own soul. His purity in my motives, His love for those I don't like, His gentleness, His wisdom. I can't tell you what a joy it is to have constant access to receive what I so desperately need from Him. Where I go for help is Romans 1:17, "For in it (the gospel) the righteousness of God is revealed from faith to faith." The key word for me here is "revealed," meaning that it takes the active work of the Holy Spirit to activate my ability to receive what I lack from my Savior. Having been forgiven from my sin, I then find that the power of sin is broken, and finally I receive the righteous life of Christ by faith.

ACCESSING GOSPEL POWER

Let's continue to unpack that verse. The "from faith to faith" part means you exercise faith in Him from day to day, situation to situation; this becomes a way of life. The rest of the verse says it well, "But the righteous man (i.e. the justified person) shall live by faith." Paul had learned to live this way by staying on the journey, praying that he might "be found in Him, not having a righteousness of my own derived from the law, but that which is through faith in Christ, the righteousness which comes from God on the basis of faith" (Philippians 3:9).

Now let's consider a real-world scenario. What can we do when we know that we ought to forgive, but we don't want to? We get stuck between the "ought" and the fact that we're not really sorry for our sin. For God to forgive us, we know that we need to repent and believe that Christ's blood atones for our sin...but here we are potentially facing two problems: we're not willing to give up our sin, and/or we don't see how we're grieving God with our sin. Whenever we find ourselves in this dilemma, we have not yet experienced repentance.

Actually, this is a common occurrence in every Christian's life; frequently we are sorrier about the consequences of a sin than sorry to God for the sin. The guilt, the loss of peace, the sense of defilement is a very bad feeling; yet to go from this condition to seriously and earnestly desiring to be free from the sin itself is a sensitivity and practice to be cultivated.

Paul gives us the classic example of inducing repentance when he writes what he deems "a severe letter" to the church in Corinth in which he strongly confronted them with their sin (2 Corinthians 6:14 - 7:1). He waited in some agony, not knowing whether they would receive his correction or refuse it. He knew that his rebuke would cause them sorrow, but he wasn't sure what type of sorrow it would be. So in this passage he contrasts two types of sorrow.

Worldly sorrow is characterized by several symptoms: feeling sorry for myself, feeling condemned but not really convicted, and feeling misunderstood and thus excusing myself. This sorrow brings discouragement and maybe even some level of depression. Paul describes that, saying that it "produces death" (2 Corinthians 7:10).

In contrast, godly sorrow comes from seeing how my sin has affected God, and it activates what Paul describes as an "earnestness," a "vindication," an "indignation," a "fear," an "avenging of wrong," that yields a dramatic turnaround or change. This is the essence of repentance (2 Corinthians 7:11), and it produces tremendous freedom!

THREE SPECIFIC APPLICATIONS

1. When caught between the "ought to" and the "don't want to," I meditate upon the scriptures that command me to not commit that particular sin. In a sense I am asking Paul to send me his letter, inviting the Holy Spirit to use the word of God to work in my will and give me the ability to repent to God.

2. James gives us a practical and effective way of coming into the Light when he writes, "Confess your sins to one another" (James 4:16). We are priests before the Lord, and we have the ability to help one another come into the life-giving Light. Personally, my wife is my priest of choice! Do you have someone who helps you?

3. Psalm 34:1 is extremely helpful. David says, "I will bless the Lord at all times." From this the Holy Spirit teaches us to invite Him into whatever we are experiencing each moment of the day. Whenever we find ourselves leaning more toward worldly sorrow than godly sorrow, take advantage of the "at all times" portion and invite Him into your soul. He really is the Helper!

Salvation is a process. We frequently say something like, "I was saved last year." And it's true; we were "saved" in a moment of time…but salvation includes the whole process of transformation to become like Christ Himself, and that goes far beyond any moment in time. Paul writes about his gospel journey, "but to us who are being saved, it (the gospel) is the power of God" (1 Corinthians 1:18). We discover in the gospel the reality of Christ to deliver us. Past, present, and future.

So we are saved in the past—that's justification. We are being saved day by day in the present—that's sanctification. And we will be saved when we receive resurrection bodies—that's glorification. All of this is salvation; all of this is the gospel. Now let's look more carefully in this next chapter at the process of character formation.

DISCUSSION QUESTIONS

1. How has your understanding of the gospel changed as a result of this chapter?

2. How would you describe the difference between the three different "powers" of the gospel?

3. In what area of your life does the power seem to be lacking right now?

4. Of the three elements of the gospel (forgiveness, power, and resurrection), which one speaks most poignantly to you at this moment? What does that message sound like?

SIX

Abiding in Christ
Forming your Character

Question: *If Christ lives within us and He is all sufficient, why do we have trouble tapping into His love, patience, wisdom, and power?* In other words, why is it so hard to live out the character of Christ in my daily life now that He has made His home inside me?

We began this conversation in the last chapter where we explored four transformational facets of gospel power in our lives. In short, the answer to our character dilemma is found in a life of constantly abiding in Christ. But before we discuss abiding, we need to understand what character development entails.

John describes our formation this way: "Beloved, now we are children of God, and it has not appeared as yet what we will be. We know that when He appears, we will be like Him, because we will see Him just as He is" (1 John 3:2). In other words we don't really know who it is we're becoming except that we are becoming more like Him! More like an authentic expression of Christ that flows through our unique souls—our one-of-a-kind personality, passions, abilities, interests. All saturated with the fragrance of heaven. That's what character is.

Character-building, just like any reconstruction project, involves both a dismantling of what doesn't belong and an installing of what does. And since God is the Architect of our souls, He knows precisely what He is crafting...and how to accomplish it. We don't so much need to understand as to follow. It is being with Him that changes us, and this is where faith plays a key role.

A FOUNDATION OF GRANITE

Jesus tells a parable in Matthew 7:24-27 that goes like this.

> Therefore everyone who hears these words of Mine and acts on them, may be compared to a wise man who built his house on the rock. And the rain fell, and the floods came, and the winds blew and slammed against that house; and yet it did not fall, for it had been founded on the rock. Everyone who hears these words of Mine and does not act on them, will be like a foolish man who built his house on the sand. The rain fell, and the floods came, and the winds blew and slammed against that house; and it fell—and great was its fall.

In this parable, Jesus compares two foundations; one doesn't work. Think of all our efforts to improve ourselves: sand. The house built down to the bedrock could sustain the fiercest of storms while the sand provided no protection whatever; no matter how beautiful the architecture, that house was going down—it was just a matter of time.

The rock could allude to many different words that Jesus spoke, but when it comes to building the "house" of our character, perhaps nothing is as foundational as the character of God. This means that, to the extent that we understand who God is (through the words of Jesus), to that extent we are building upon a solid foundation. And not just who God is in Himself, but who He is in relationship to us.

How did David do it? "This I know, that God is for me" (Psalm 56:9b). This is the epicenter of David's reality, the core truth of his world; everything else rests upon this! The essential goodness of God must be more than an abstraction; it has to be personal. God's goodness must show up in my life consistently and reliably. At a primal level, we can never give ourselves unreservedly to someone that we do not trust. And at the center of life, we join David in affirming God's unwavering commitment to us. To me. This is bedrock.

God loves me. He enjoys me. He delights in me, is crazy about me, thinks about me constantly and seeks my good in every single situation. He is 100% worthy of our trust, even in the midst of a rather high level of pain and suffering in the world. Until we know that we know this, the formation of our character will be undermined continually by other messages about who God is and who we are. This truth and experience is the anchor of our souls.

Why is this so important? Because God's crafting of character involves two powerful forces in our lives: breaking our wills and winning our hearts. And both of these require trust.

BROKENNESS: THE SOLUTION TO PRIDE

The human soul contains a will—a proud and stubborn commitment to what we want, what we believe will make us happy. If you have parented a child through the "terrible twos," then you know the drill. Your child's "No, I don't want to" is a less-refined version of our own resistance.

Picture a mustang running wild on the western prairies. He follows his instincts and answers to no one. He will run or fight to have it his way, and this is a snapshot of our human wills. God's good intent is to break this "horse's" will so that the Master can saddle, bridle, and ride him. He wants to break our wills, not our spirits. Once broken to the master's will, we can become so sensitive to His desire, that the merest shift of weight will cause us to respond and turn left, right, even back up. This is the intimacy for which our hearts truly long.

Roy Hession describes the type of brokenness Jesus desires for His disciples:

> The Lord Jesus cannot live in us fully and reveal Himself through us until the proud self within us is broken. This simply means that the hard unyielding self, which justifies itself, wants its own way, stands up for its rights, and seeks its own glory, at last bows its head to God's will, admits it's wrong, gives up its own way to Jesus, surrenders its right and discards its own glory—that the Lord Jesus might have all and be all. In other words, it is dying to self and self-attitudes (*Calvary Road*, p.20).

Hession does a great job of identifying our emotions that reveal our resistance to Christ's will. "It is always self who gets irritable and

81

envious and resentful and critical and worried.... It is self who is shy and self-conscious, and reserved." We need to learn to spot the feelings that reveal our unbrokenness, which lies at the heart of our failure to receive God's sufficiency at all times.

He mentions other such feelings: self-pity, self-indulgence, sensitiveness, touchiness, resentment, self-defense, grumbling, bossiness, carelessness, jealousy...not to mention excusing ourselves or blaming others (p. 26,29). How about our insecurities? More "sand." We all suffer with basic fears about our worth, our identity, how we seem to others. All of this comes from self-dependence rather than depending upon Christ, our "Rock."

Jesus is the only Man we have as a model of one whose will was fully and completely submitted to God. This is not natural to us. Our entire culture and education flies in the face of this: our world is anti-brokenness. Only those who follow Jesus come to appreciate the value of having their wills broken—another expression for the theological term "sanctification" that we discussed in the last chapter.

WOOING: THE SOLUTION TO FEAR

While brokenness is the solution to our proud, stubborn wills, we are more than our wills. We also have a heart that longs to be loved, pursued, and desired. It is essential to grasp that even as God uses circumstances to place boundaries and constraints around our independence, he also uses a thousand voices to communicate His undying love and affection for us.

Consider again the beloved Psalm 23 that likens God to a good shepherd—One committed to provide for us, quiet us, restore us, and guide us. One who extends His powerful stewardship over our lives to comfort and protect us from evil. To feed us. To invite us to rule with Him and share His goodness forever.

David references the standard tools of the trade in shepherding— His rod and staff comfort us. The character formation He is after in our lives (that which we so keenly need in order to come into the fullness of our calling) requires both correction and protection. This is why the

Father dismantles the destructive power of our wills even while He woos our hearts as the most tender of Lovers.

What's more, different soul structures need more of one and less of the other, which allows God to customize His work in our lives to our unique soul structure. Not only that, different seasons of life call for more of one and less of the other. Only God can know us so intimately and provide for us so thoroughly!

A nasty sidekick to pride is fear—and we are well familiar with both these imposters. The root of both is a lack of trust in the goodness of the Shepherd, which takes us full circle back to the shepherd boy's declaration in another of his songs: *This I know, that God is for me!* If He is to mold and shape the form of our character into the image of His Son, He must constrain our impulse to bolt and win our trust to come near. The result: what John the disciple calls "abiding."

ABIDING: THE PATH TO TRANSFORMATION

As the Architect of our souls, God knows how to break our wills and to win our hearts. And as we break free of the grip that fear and pride exert upon us, we approach that joyful place in relationship to God that is called "abiding in Christ" in John 15. This is both the destination and the path of our journey. This is *Doing Life With*. This is what we are made for.

The picture of a vine represents the constant flow of life and vitality directed to us. The "branches" tell us that we are attached to Him as our source. We know what it is to participate in the unbroken flow...and we also know what it feels like to detach ourselves and begin to wither and dry up on the inside.

Abiding in Christ is the practical day-to-day experience of what God did when He placed us in Christ before the foundation of the world (Ephesians 1:4). Everything we receive from God comes to us in, because of, and through our union with Christ. Many genuine Christians know and believe these truths yet lack understanding about how to live in the reality of what God offers us through abiding.

As Andrew Murray points out, many feel unqualified to abide in Him. Many look at this picture longingly but immediately face inner challenges: 1) *I can never quite get there.* 2) *I don't know how.* 3) *This must be for the special people who are more spiritual than I am.*

So let's back up and take another look at how Jesus related to His Father. As the model Son, He showed us what it looks like to rest and rely upon God fully. This is how He received inspiration, power, love, and every ability that life required from Him.

John really captured this dynamic in Jesus' life, culminating in the vine-and-branch imagery; listen to his insights here.

- Jesus says, "I have food to eat that you do not know about," referring to His feeding upon Father's love and sustaining power (John 4:32).

- Later he puts it this way: "The Son can do nothing of Himself, unless it is something He sees the Father doing; for whatever the Father does, these things the Son also does in like manner. For the Father loves the Son, and shows Him all things that He Himself is doing" (John 5:19-20).

- When Jesus describes how He lives, He explains, "the Father abiding in Me does His works" (John 14:10b).

Jesus isn't relying upon Himself but is working with Father as the One who initiates and leads so that Jesus can simply do life *with* Father. God desires to be *with* us. This is the meaning of Isaiah's prophetic word for Him, "Immanuel," God with us (Isaiah 7:14). Jesus demonstrates what it's like to live with this level of intimacy in Father's love. This keen sense that "the Son can do nothing of Himself" is the basis of both humility and faith.

APPLICATIONS: ACCESSING THE PATH

Abiding is the path toward character formation, and we are invited by Jesus to abide in Him, just like a branch thrives in relationship with the Vine. *What does that path look like in daily life?* Well, it can look a lot of different ways, but here are a few common practices for daily abiding:

Living in the love. We've already looked at the depth of David's and Jesus' revelation of God's ongoing affection and commitment in their lives. You'll be hard-pressed to find any of the biblical heroes and heroines of faith who didn't live out of this overarching reality, and in the next chapter we'll go into great detail about how to cultivate a thriving devotional life with God so that love becomes the paramount experience of being a Christ-follower.

But for now, make it a habit to live each day as the beloved of God. It's an internal posture, a fixed identity unshakable by circumstance. Start each day by actively receiving the love of God. Without this anchor of the soul, nothing else works.

Embracing weakness. Paul beautifully describes the challenge and reward of tapping into God's power through his weaknesses.

> He has said to me, "My grace is sufficient for you, for power is perfected in weakness." Most gladly, therefore, I will rather boast about my weaknesses, so that the power of Christ may dwell in me. Therefore I am well content with weaknesses, with insults, with distresses, with persecutions, with difficulties, for Christ's sake; for when I am weak, then I am strong (2 Corinthians 12:9-10).

Clearly, this advice cuts directly across every human instinct. Weakness and lack of control is what we often fear most in our lives, but Paul calls us to live in this place of abandonment and absolute trust. As long as we're intent on forming ourselves, His power is switched off, and we merely frustrate ourselves. "As the branch cannot bear fruit of itself unless it abides in the vine, so neither can you unless you abide in Me" (John 15:4-5). Abiding is sweet surrender. You will want to reflect upon this every day until it becomes part of who you are.

Insecurity. Pressure. Worry. Drivenness. These are the dashboard warning lights that let us know when we have stopped abiding and are trying to work out of our own human resources. It's a great system!

When we strive, we begin to shrivel and die inside; when we abide, the joy and sufficiency flow in spades. Don't be discouraged when you see yourself shriveling. If you are noticing it, then you are making progress because this is part of how the Spirit teaches you. It takes lots of rounds of this for us to lean more intentionally into the abiding.

Choosing rest. To abide in Christ means to depend upon Him for your sufficiency and adequacy—living in what Hebrews calls *His rest*. "For the one who has entered His rest has himself also rested from his works, as God did from His. Therefore let us be diligent to enter that rest" (Hebrews 4:10). This passage calls us to stop trying to perform, stop trying to live the Christian life in our own effort; instead, there is this compelling invitation to enter into a life in which Jesus has done it all for us and we merely participate in His life. It's a choice.

Getting out of rest is how we learn to recognize that our stubborn will is engaged. Surrendering our wills to Him is a lifetime process, and it happens best within a vision to simply abide in Christ.

Andrew Murray describes abiding as, "The soul has only to yield itself to Him, to be still and to rest in the confidence that His love has undertaken, and that His faithfulness will perform, the work of keeping it safe" (*Abiding in Christ*, p.22). Amen.

Partnering with the Holy Spirit. In Philippians 3:12-13 Paul writes that Jesus "laid hold" of him and that he responds by "laying hold" of Christ. This is some fresh language to describe the partnering quality of abiding. God acts first—and we act in response to God. So abiding is clearly initiated by Him, yet it is not a passive dynamic on our part. Rather, we are to actively "remain in His love," as John puts it (John 15:10).

It is in the love-response of saying *yes* to God's *yes* that we integrate ourselves fully into the Vine of his formation. It is as we actively draw upon the "sap" of His life that we are transformed in our character to look more like Father in our own being and doing. It is also as we abide in Him that the Father tends us, trimming off the parts of our lives that are dead weight and catalyzing the parts that are healthy toward growth (John 15:1).

Repenting as a lifestyle. The Bible word for describing this pruning process is repentance, and in the life of one who is abiding, it is an unexpectedly joyful process. Yes, there is a death of sorts, and it can involve some pain, but it is *a death to death* and invariably brings with it a profound sense of relief as the weight of sin falls away and the loving presence of the Vinekeeper is renewed in our lives.

Our part in responding to the pruning looks like this:

1. Come into the light. (1 John 1:7, "But if we walk in the light, as he is in the light, we have fellowship with one another, and the blood of Jesus, his Son, purifies us from all sin.")

2. Identify with Christ at the cross. (Galatians 2:20, "I have been crucified with Christ and I no longer live, but Christ lives in me. The life I now live in the body, I live by faith in the Son of God, who loved me and gave himself for me.")

3. Enter right back into restored fellowship with the Father.

Walking with God, spending time with God, walking in the Spirit by staying sensitive to Him and agreeing with Him in our attitudes, words and choices: this is the normal way of life for us as we abide.

When David deeply repented in Psalm 51, he expressed God's heart most accurately: "Behold, You desire truth in the innermost being.... Create in me a clean heart, O God." This, as we discussed in the last chapter, is the very process that activates the Power of the Blood.

Living as a servant. In his book, *The Five Love Languages*, Gary Chapman describes five ways in which spouses can express love for one another: words of affirmation, acts of service, physical touch, quality time, and gifts. Of these five, serving has proven to be the most challenging for me. And I suspect I am not alone in this; in our humanity, we are much more interested in *being served* than in serving others. Jesus had to correct this fallacy among His disciples frequently. His words on this point are clear and strong:

> But do not be called Rabbi; for One is your Teacher, and you are all brothers. Do not call anyone on earth your father; for One is your Father, He who is in heaven. Do not be called

leaders; for One is your Leader, that is, Christ. But the greatest among you shall be your servant. Whoever exalts himself shall be humbled; and whoever humbles himself shall be exalted (Matthew 23:8-12).

In direct contrast to our human instincts, Jesus came to earth as a Servant. In fact, He defined His leadership as being a servant. Listen to Roy Hession describe 5 marks of living the servant life (*Calvary Road*, p. 73-75):

1. He must be willing to have one thing on top of another put upon him without any consideration being given him.

2. He must be willing not to be thanked for it.

3. He must not charge the other with selfishness.

4. Having done all that, there is no ground for pride or self-congratulation, but we must confess that we are unprofitable servants.

5. The admission that doing and bearing what we have in the way of meekness and humility, we have not done one stich more than it was our duty to do.

Strengthening one another. While we Protestants rightly insist that we don't have to confess our sins to a priest, we often overlook an important principle in James 5:16, which calls us to confess our sins to one another. Rather than having one priest in the church, we are all priests and are to minister to one another (1 Peter 2:9). So we have a powerful opportunity to build relationships of mutual trust and transparency through the spiritual practice of confession. This is one reason I don't call myself "Pastor Jerry" because while I may be the leader, all God's people are pastors.

Confession lays the groundwork for the legitimate practice of *accountability*. Those who are willing to open themselves to trustworthy souls find that such accountability fuels their spiritual growth in powerful ways. Overbearing leaders have too often manipulated confession to their own advantage, making it into a tool of shame and control. Of course, this is the very antithesis of God's intent. Instead, accountability is meant to be a force for calling one another into our true redeemed selves and empowering one other toward the character and calling of Christ.

The truth is that very few church leaders practice biblical accountability. There may be lip service to the concept, but few actually submit their lives and actions to a mentor or community for group discernment. When leading a church, I practice one level of accountability to the elders (and require it also of them) and an even deeper level with my wife on a daily basis.

What does this look like? With elders I regularly ask key questions: *Are you praying daily with your wife? Have you watched any pornography? Is there anyone you have not forgiven?* I may switch up the questions from time to time, but I ask them and answer them first myself. If no one is asking you questions like these on a regular basis, you can instigate it! Volunteer your own accountability and then invite theirs.

This is equally true in your marriage. Nan and I begin our day with shared devotions. She is always invited to read my journal at any time, and she often does. We confess our sins before God and with one another. We keep no secrets, and therefore we are mutually accountable.

How can we live more this way? We are safe with our Father. He never condemns us (Romans 8:1). Jesus is our Advocate (1 John 2:1). He only uses guilt to draw us into His love that forgives and cleanses us. Living in this safety is so life-giving. We are safe there.

We are also safe with one another when we live with this kind of transparency, and in this way we advocate for one another. In this way we remind ourselves to stay plugged into the life of the Vine, and we encourage those with whom we are in relationship to remain equally connected to the flow of God. Abiding in Christ daily is the path to transformation of character.

DISCUSSION QUESTIONS

1. What is your experience of abiding in Christ?

2. What do you find most challenging in this day-to-day abiding?

3. What does "entering His rest" look like in your life?

SEVEN

Carving Out Your Drop Zone
Thriving in Your Devotional Life

The rhythmic chop of the helicopter echoed across the hills as the pilot came in low, his eyes quickly taking in the drop zone, scanning for enemy fire. Tracers started flying, and he instinctively pulled back on the stick, ducking back out over the hill. Meanwhile, you are on the ground below, waiting for essential supplies. Bad guys coming, ammo low, and...you watch the chopper swoosh away. Talk about a bad feeling!

From 1965 through 1967 I served three tours as a pilot in Vietnam. Flying a Lockheed EC-121 AWACS aircraft, our mission was to provide early-warning radar surveillance using two large radomes, a vertical dome above the fuselage and a horizontal one below it. By tracking the enemy's movement, we were able to direct fighter aircraft to the appropriate threats.

When it came to ground support, however, many of our engaged units could only be supplied by helicopters that could land in the dense jungle terrain. Picture a company of soldiers that has secured a hilltop in its mission to pacify the area. Everything that company needs— food, water, ammunition, mail, casualty transport—comes in by air. There is no other access.

So what if the helicopters can't land? Well, then the troops go without! It's the responsibility of the guys on the ground to carve out the jungle and secure the perimeter, making it reasonably safe for a chopper to get in and out. There's an old military saying that "an army marches on its stomach." No food, no ammo, no fight. It's called interdiction, and it's why Hitler lost his battles in Russia toward the end of the second World War: they could not reliably equip and support their troops on the ground.

So what about you? How functional is your drop zone?

Just like those ground troops, everything you need for spiritual health, supply, and sustenance comes from above. Healing of wounds, soul nourishment, wisdom and discernment, fresh passion, comfort, insight, perspective—everything you need is supplied supernaturally through Christ.

I wonder if right here you might relate securing your perimeter to securing your time with God each morning…and relate carving out a landing zone to going to bed early enough to make that morning meeting with God work.

But what if you don't take the time to receive your spiritual supplies? In short, you go hungry…and your battle effectiveness is diminished day by day. Many well-intentioned believers essentially wind up in a spiritual coma—technically alive but completely out of the fight. Hurting and ineffective because they lack the provision their souls so desperately crave. We have all experienced this dynamic at some point in our journey. Maybe this describes you right now.

BEING WITH

Where is God in your daily schedule? Is that time secured? Something will always be first in our day, so if it isn't God, it's something else. Something that may *feel* more urgent, more pressing, but is not actually more important. Really, nothing is as important to our well-being over the long run than our daily connection with God.

Hear me on this: the life Jesus calls us to is an impossible one! It is completely inaccessible to us in our humanity. It involves a cross. It involves forgiving our friends and loving our enemies. It calls for humility. It calls us to a life without worry and fear. A life of relational commitment. Essentially, it's so supernatural that most people don't even take these commands very seriously. When we do take them seriously, we find that we need some serious horsepower beyond what's under our own hood…and that's what the spiritual drop zone is all about.

So before we dive in to explore how to receive personally from God, let's take a quick look at the example of Christ. How did Jesus live, and what did He model in terms of his own drop zone? When we look through these glasses, we discover Jesus' secret: doing life intimately connected with His Father.

John 5:19-21 finds Jesus describing this crucial interdependency. In essence he says, *I can't pull this off on my own. My life as a Son requires me to constantly pay attention to what my Father is up to. And because He loves me, he is always giving me clear directions on how to cooperate with His game plan.* Can you see how Jesus was tapping into a steady supply of heavenly resources? (Also John 8:29; 14:10b). He was modeling this for us as well.

When Jesus called His disciples, the call was to be *with Him*. To live with Him, eat and sleep with Him, travel with Him and watch Him work. This was on-the-job training at its finest! No formal classroom time whatsoever. And this approach to disciple-making resulted in a high level of intimacy. So Jesus' plan for supplying a drop zone to His disciples was simply "being with" (see John 5:39-40).

This is how divine guidance works: "Rabbi, where are you staying?" "Come and see. By being with me, you'll see how this works!" (John 1:39) Listen to Jesus' conversation with Thomas: "You know the way," Jesus says. "No, I really don't" is Thomas' reply. "I am the Way" (John 14:4-5). Jesus has one condition for prospective disciples—come and do life with Me! (John 1:4) The American church has confused things by defining a Christian as Forgiven rather than Follower. Receiving forgiveness is just the beginning, just the invitation.

So the pattern is clear. Jesus looked to the Father for regular supply in His drop zone. And then Jesus guided His disciples to relate to Him the same way—regular supply through their own individual drop zones. It's no different for us. The destiny of your life hinges on carving out time and place to truly be *with Him* as well.

A RADICAL OFFER

So here's a radical thought: what if you could start your life all over and build it on this word of Jesus to you: "Come to Me, all who are weary and heavy-laden, and I will give you rest. Take My yoke upon you and learn from Me, for I am gentle and humble in heart, and you will find rest for your souls. For My yoke is easy and My burden is light" (Matthew 11:28-30). Now is that an invitation or what? We trade in our heavy load of fear, worry, obligation, and performance in return for, well, the opposite. Jesus called it "rest," and it's a pretty expansive offering.

The author of Hebrews describes rest (or "Sabbath rest") as a participation in God's rest—both in creation and in re-creation. Rest is finding in Jesus His ability and His power to be adequate, to forgive, to be wise, and to obtain everything we need. Rest is finding in Jesus our identity, our worth, and our acceptance. Trying to achieve this ourselves is both exhausting and fruitless.

The reason that things were not going well for the Hebrew Christians was that they weren't living in this rest. They were still trying to accomplish and achieve on their own dime. And we can well relate.

What does Jesus mean when he urges us to "take My yoke upon you and learn of Me"? A yoke binds two animals together—perhaps a young, weak ox together with a strong, mature ox so they can work in tandem. In our case, this is Jesus' call to us to do life together. It is the "abiding in Christ" that He calls us to in the parable of the vine. It's staying dependent upon Him, relying upon His sufficiency.

A yoke is a high-trust operation, so Jesus tells us what He's like so we will never be afraid of how we will be treated. He's gentle. He's humble. There is an "ease" to being and working with Him. What makes His yoke easy? It's easy because you are drawing all your life and energy, your stamina, wisdom, and abilities, all your guidance, finances, and timing directly from Him.

This yoke is a learning environment. What does He want you to learn? To learn Him, His ways, His nature. And to actually receive His nature into you. This is how learning takes place, and this is the essence of being with Him. When we do this, we not only hear His promise of rest, we actually receive that rest into the deep place inside. "You will find rest for your souls!" is His promise that assures us it's not just theoretical; it's practical.

Listen to Him again: He says, *I am your bread, your water, your source of love, your soul-restoration, your grace hook-up. Every single day will make you weary with worries, concerns, fears, guilt, pressures, and endless responsibilities...but I teach my children how to take advantage of their weaknesses* (see 2 Corinthians 12:9-10).

DROP ZONE LOGISTICS

So we're saying yes to this radical offer, right? We're ready to discard our striving and failing and step into yoke with Him for this intimate experience of living and working in rest. But what are the practicalities of setting up the drop zone?

When you read the Psalms, you find a recurring theme: morning.

"In the morning, O Lord, you will hear my voice" (5:3). "I shall joyfully sing of Your lovingkindness in the morning" (59:16). "In the morning my prayer comes before You" (88:13). "O satisfy us in the morning with Your lovingkindness, that we may sing for joy and be glad all our days" (90:14).

There is something powerful about turning our first thoughts, our first attention, toward God in the day. About stepping into that identity and that yoke of mutual participation first thing. It is an orientation to the day that allows us to abide and to rest most effectively. It can also be challenging to put into practice.

There are two roadblocks I usually run into: time pressures and performance pressures. *When will I find the time?* we lament. But time management is a misnomer. Nobody manages time; time manages to roll on like clockwork without any need for external management. Instead, we manage (or don't manage) our priorities. Carving out our drop zone in the morning only happens when its priority moves up the ladder.

Ultimately, we don't find time; we make it. And that requires a high level of motivation, even desperation. If you are not setting aside an hour to start your day with Jesus, then you must believe you can accomplish more by using that time doing stuff on your own. This is part of the cost of discipleship...but we also need to understand *the cost of non-discipleship*! Without our daily drop zone we spin our wheels, kicking up an impressive cloud of dust with our efforts but eventually realizing that it's not really working. I know disciples who are getting up at 4:00 or 4:30 am in order to have time with Him. Why do they do this? Because they are convinced they cannot make it on their own.

It can be difficult, of course, particularly depending upon your job requirements. Some jobs have people working in the night or at odd shifts or—toughest of all—rotating schedules that are different every week! Sometimes we have to adapt our drop zone to whatever "morning" marks the beginning of our work day. But it can be done. It must be done!

Many times performance pressures outweigh even the time pressures we face. "I've tried that and failed. I don't want to tell my wife that we are going to carve out this particular time in the morning…and then fail again!" Sometimes it's easier not to try than to run that risk. But here's the deal: we need to change the rules and establish a climate where it's safe to fail. This is an entirely new mindset for many.

Failing is perhaps the most important part of our learning and growth. Few things train us like experience, so we have to make a culture shift here and realize that we often find a lot of things *that don't work*…before we find what does. These are the right kind of "failures"—experiments to discover what works.

NAVIGATING THE SEASONS

On my first deployment to Vietnam, I was rooming with three other Lieutenants who all happened to be drunks; we would awaken at 12:30am for our missions, and there was nowhere else to go for devotions other than kneeling down at my bed. The other men would be stumbling around, cursing and carrying on, but I was desperate for my drop zone. Some would call this discipline; I call it my lifeline.

We all go through seasons of life—times when things change. Like the change from Vietnam to our home in California. The rhythms and routines of life get shaken up and have to adapt to new patterns. When this happens, we have to carve out the drop zone in a new way; we may have to modify times, places, and strategies to work within a new framework. Just because the context changes doesn't mean that we need his daily supernatural supply any less. If anything, we need it more in the intrinsic stress of change.

When our children were young, we had an hour of devotions before the children were up. Breakfast and school came later. Now, with children long out of the nest, we eat breakfast first and then take the next hour and a half for this time.

We sit in our little devotions spot, a couple comfortable chairs in a corner of our room that feels like a spiritual home. We both begin by journaling, which for me really connects me with God. Maybe it's because I'm a visual learner, but writing down the emotions I'm feeling and sharing this with my Father on paper is crucial for me. Years ago we started by reading Spurgeon's devotional, but now journaling has become my first point of connection. Then I do what I learned from George Muller: I ask the Holy Spirit to speak to me from Scripture. I read my Bible with pen & marker.

Your dynamic may be different from mine, and that's the beauty of meeting with God. We have many of the same tools, but by following the Spirit's prompt, we can adapt God's resources to the unique needs of our spiritual season. Over time, I have changed some aspects of what I do. My principle is to follow the Life.

We are always in Christ's school because He's always teaching us something. This year I've found life in praying through the Psalms before I dig into the New Testament. Recently the Spirit has prompted me to spend time just being still and listening. There are times when the Holy Spirit draws close to me in memorizing or meditating upon scripture. Sometimes it's waiting on God; sometimes it's singing and worship.

Nan and I usually share back and forth scriptures, insights, and struggles during the next portion of time so that when we actually begin to pray, we are on the same page. I confess my sins to God in front of Nan, and she does the same. It's important for us to receive His presence and help in our own lives first before we begin to pray for others. We may pray over a promise or revelation that the Spirit has specifically quickened to us.

Then we usually make time to intercede for our family, the people we mentor, other pastors, missionaries, and friends. This early morning time spent coming to Him and being with Him tunes us into the Holy Spirit so we can walk with Him throughout the rest of the day. This time of intercession frequently spills over and carries through into other times of work, exercise, eating, and rest. For example I don't generally listen to music in the car; instead, this is often a time to pray and listen. In that sense, a devotional time becomes a devotional life.

THE HEART OF THE DISCIPLINES

As we broaden our understanding of receiving from God each day in our personal "drop zone," the next topic to explore is the spiritual disciplines. Frankly, these were so well known in Jesus' day that there was little need for Him to teach on them. Prayer, fasting, meditation, memorization, solitude, simplicity, intercession, waiting on God, listening, tithing—the Jewish community was already familiar with these. Modern-day America, however, is not.

Paul wrote to Timothy, urging him to "gymnasium yourself unto godliness" (1 Timothy 4:7). Our versions say, "discipline yourself," but the concept came from the world of athletics. He continues, "For bodily 'gymnasium' is only of little profit, but godliness is profitable for all things, since it holds promise for the present life and also for the life to come" (1 Timothy 4:8). So Paul relates the act of regularly practicing and pushing our spiritual lives to that of physical exercise, saying that it produces benefit both in our earthly lives as well as our eternal state.

Before we delve into the disciplines themselves, we need to establish the source and heart of these practices. Doing life with God is rooted in the first of all virtues: humility. Without this foundation of character, the disciplines can injure rather than strengthen the soul.

Why humility? Pride, self-sufficiency, self-dependency, and independence are all direct rebukes to God. Pride is the original sin and the starting point of every sin. Every relationship problem can be traced back to pride, usually in both parties. Since the grace of God is the only cure for sin, the Holy Spirit uniquely targets our pride in His course of Spiritual Formation 101. If God is going to save us, He must start (and continue for a lifetime) to save us from the inner workings of our pride.

Listen to some words of scripture on this topic: "The Lord will tear down the house of the proud" (Proverbs 15:25). "God is opposed to the proud, but gives grace to the humble" (1 Peter 5:5). "Whoever wishes to become great among you shall be your servant, and whoever wishes to be first among you shall be your slave" (Matthew 20:16-18).

And then there was Jesus. Jesus' incarnation is God's last word about humility! "Have this attitude in yourselves which was also in Christ Jesus, who, although, He existed in the form of God, did not regard equality with God a thing to be grasped, but emptied Himself taking the form of a bond-servant, and being made in the likeness of men. He humbled Himself by becoming obedient to the point of death" (Philippians 2:5-8).

The reason Satan could not gain any access in Jesus' very human soul was His humility. His whole relationship with His Father was based on His humility. "The Son can do nothing of Himself, unless it is something He sees the Father doing; for whatever the Father does, these things the Son also does in like manner." (John 5:19; see also John 5:30, 44).

It was Jesus' humility that allowed Him to fully experience the Father working through him day after day (see John 14:10). Our relationship with God the Father cannot go deeper or be realized any more fully than our humility allows. In fact, the kingdom of God is defined as any place where God's authority is recognized and submitted to. This is humility!

Nothing in Jesus resisted living underneath the Father's authority; therefore, He was the perfect conduit for God's authority to be expressed through Him! Jesus came to inaugurate God's rule (His kingdom) on the earth. This is why He called the gospel "the gospel of the kingdom" (Matthew 4:23; 9:35; 29:14) and naturally He starts by teaching on humility (Matthew 5:3).

"Who is greatest in the kingdom?" Jesus' disciples inquire of him. His answer: "Whoever then humbles himself" (Matthew 18:1,3). The Man with perfect humility practiced the spiritual disciplines, and no one can successfully follow Him without a lifestyle of similar practices.

THE STUDY OF SCRIPTURE

As the presence of God intersects with our growing humility, we are instinctively drawn toward the spiritual disciplines themselves. Bible study is often the first spiritual discipline in a disciple's experience, and Jesus made it clear that studying His words was an essential part of being His student. "If you continue in My word, then you are truly My disciples; and you will know the truth, and the truth will make you free" (John 8:31-32).

Jesus spent His childhood studying Scripture and integrating it into His heart and mind (Luke 2:46-47). How much study, memorization, meditation, waiting on God, and prayer do we think He must have done by the age of twelve? A sizeable amount! These practices must have been forged into the core of His life.

Bible study is a discipline because it's more than a casual read through a book. Yet while it's a discipline, it is also a learned skill. It involves reading a book so as to discover why the author wrote it, what his overall message is, and how each paragraph or sentence logically fits into the author's purpose.

Once we understand that, then we get to apply those messages to our own journey. The Holy Spirit wrote the words to readers thousands of years ago, and we sometimes forget that God is speaking to our lives today using the subjects, verbs, objects, modifiers, prepositions, tenses, and moods of those original words. So the study of those words gives us powerful access to the wisdom and love and guidance of God. As a mentor, you can help those you lead draw God's message from Scripture by asking the right questions. Another useful technique is to ask a disciple to rewrite a passage in his own words.

Practically speaking, I always read my Bible with my marking pen and highlighter in hand. I underline key words, phrases, names— whatever catches my attention and inspires me. Because I am a visual learner, I interact with the text by writing my responses, insights, and questions in the margin. I use a Study Bible and often reread the introductions to remind me when, where, and to whom a book was written.

Of course, there are myriads of Bible translations; chose a translation that speaks to you. Read a different translation every year. Personally, I prefer a more word-accurate translation such as the New American Standard Version (NASV) or English Standard Version (ESV). Keep notes in your Bible. Date the promises that God gives you as you read. You can also create categories in the back of your Bible and record verses over the years that relate to those subjects.

MORE DISCIPLINES

Let's look at some of the other spiritual disciplines. The study of scripture is a great starting point, but it doesn't stop there. We can use these same scriptures in even more ways that spark growth and devotion—memorization, meditation, and prayer to name a few.

Scripture Memorization. David says, "How can a young man keep his way pure? By keeping it according to Your word. Your word I have hidden [treasured] in my heart, that I may not sin against You" (Psalm 119:9,11). This act of treasuring God's word in the heart begins by memorizing key passages.

This is an essential practice for transforming our minds, reprogramming the way we think and respond to life situations. The Holy Spirit often speaks to us by bringing to our minds the right verse when we need it. The more scripture that is embedded in our hearts, the greater the reservoir from which the Spirit can draw and activate.

Meditation. Memorization sets the stage for meditation—rolling the words of God around in our spirit and letting them sink deep into our souls. Meditation is like a cow chewing its cud; the food cycles around numerous times, continuing to yield nutrition and giving the cow the maximum benefit of its food. Meditation is similar for us.

Sometimes the Spirit of God takes me into a season of weeks or months of meditation. In those times I spend lengthy periods just reading one or two verses over and over and over, turning every word over in my mind, letting it settle inside my head and my heart. David describes a righteous man as one who delights in God's law and meditates on it day and night. As a result, "He will be like a tree firmly planted by streams of water, which yields its fruit in its season" (Psalm 1:2-3).

Prayer. This powerful practice covers a broad range of disciplines and can be one of the most personal ways of connecting and communing with God. Drawing near to God is part of prayer: "Therefore let us draw near with confidence to the throne of grace, so that we may receive mercy and find grace to help in time of need" (Hebrews 4:16).

We want to teach others how to come through Christ in order to be with Father and experience His presence. Here are a few practical points in this process:

- First, learn to draw directly from God—His love, His forgiveness, His approval, His comfort, His wisdom (1 John 1:7,9; Jam.1:2-5).

- Second, come to Jesus according to His invitation—to sense the personal welcome of Christ (Matthew 11:28-30).

- Next, teach your disciple how to abide in Christ, which is the key to fruitfulness in our lives (John 15). Read through Andrew Murray's 31-day devotional, *Abide in Christ*.

Many Christians know the concept of abiding but have no idea how to actually do it. Murray will help. I like to link the message of abiding with 2 Corinthians 12:9, 10, learning to use my weaknesses as the way to fully rely upon Him.

Abiding in Christ isn't limited to prayer. However, drawing near to Him and by faith relying upon Him alone during prayer equips your heart and mind to walk with Him throughout the day. Remember the instructions we get before a plane flight? Put on your own oxygen mask first; then help others with theirs. Before you intercede for others (which is important) you must get your own soul fed, and the way you do that is to feed upon Christ Himself. Jesus showed us the way, saying, "I have food to eat that you do not know about" (John 4:32). Fortunately, we have access to the same spiritual buffet He did.

Praying Scripture. One specific application of prayer takes us right back to scripture, finding God's own words to be another transformational point of connection. Because these passages embody both the experiences of those spiritual pilgrims who have gone before us, as well as God's response to them, we can "go to school" on these truths and appropriate them for our own journey in God.

Pray through the Psalms. Read a phrase or a verse, echoing the same words as an expression of your heart to God, and then speak what the Spirit brings out of the verse back to Him. In this way, we enlarge our spiritual "vocabulary" with God. We also are leveraging the learnings of David and the many other biblical writers.

Praying God's promises is another way of activating and owning biblical truth. Paul reminds us that "for no matter how many promises God has made, they are 'Yes' in Christ, and so through Him the 'Amen' is spoken by us to the glory of God" (2 Corinthians 1:20 NIV). Peter agrees: "Through these He has given us His very great and precious promises, so that through them you may participate in the divine nature and escape the corruption in the world caused by evil desires" (2 Peter 1:3 NIV).

Abraham became the father of our faith by honoring God and reminding Him of His promise. "Yet, with respect to the promise of God, he did not waver in unbelief but grew strong in faith, giving glory to God" (Romans 4:20). We too have this ongoing invitation to personally own and apply the character of God reflected in His many promises in scripture.

Private worship. Personal praise and worship is a particularly intimate way to commune with God, using "psalms and hymns and spiritual songs" (Ephesians 5:19) to declare who God is, remember what He has done, and convey the adoration of our hearts toward Him. Corporate worship affirms our solidarity with the faith community before God. Private worship affirms His individual lordship in our lives.

Conversely, stillness and silence before God is another expression of worship. "Be still and know I am God" (Psalm 46:10 KJV). We'll explore that a bit more in a moment.

"Delight yourself in the Lord; and He will give you the desires of your heart" (Psalm 37:4). This is worship. "Ascribe to the Lord, O sons of the mighty, ascribe to the Lord glory and strength" (Psalm 29:1). This is worship. Essentially, there are dozens of creative ways to authentically engage with God out of a worshipful heart. It is a vital practice for every disciple.

Waiting upon the Lord is an expression of worship that says that He is the Initiator, the Source, and that we depend fully on Him. David says, "I waited patiently for the Lord; and He inclined to me and heard my cry" (Psalm 40:1). *Waiting On God* by Andrew Murray is an excellent source to unpack the potential of this spiritual discipline.

One of the highest forms of worship is "ministering to the Lord," which we see practiced in Acts 13:2. God is in relationship with us, and we get to minister to Him by loving on Him and expressing our interest in Him.

Another high form of worship is praising God when we are hurting. Worship leader Matt Redman calls this "pain in the offering." This uniquely costly worship seems to receive special regard by God in the scriptures, and of course that's because it is counter-intuitive. Our natural reaction in pain is to feel unprotected by God and then either accuse or ignore Him. Instead, worship from a place of suffering becomes the most precious form of trust.

Intercession. This discipline shifts the attention from ourselves to others. Now that we have fed deeply and richly on Christ for our own souls, we can advocate for others. Paul made it clear how important it is to pray for those we love and serve. (1 Timothy 2:1-3) Paul also makes an appeal for others to pray for him, "Pray on my behalf, that utterance maybe given to me in the opening of my mouth, to make known with boldness the mystery of the gospel" (Ephesians 6:19).

We also recognize that prayer is spiritual warfare, as James reminds us: "Submit to God, resist the devil, and he will flee" (4:7). And Paul uses an expansive metaphor in Ephesians 6, describing the armor provided for us in spiritual warfare. He says that in prayer we take our place as "seated with Christ" (Ephesians 2:6) and use our faith to assert Christ's victory and authority over the devil.

We are also charged to pray without ceasing. I find that investing an hour or an hour and a half in Scripture and prayer sets me up to pray as I proceed with my days' activities. Whatever you do—going to get the newspaper, driving a car, reading emails—make prayer part of it. Pray over appointments. Pray for friends as you shop. Personally, I often pray in tongues, and I constantly pray for the nine gifts of the Spirit so that I might be able to minister to anyone I meet.

Journaling. The practice of journaling helps to "locate your soul." This is where I begin my devotional times. Taking my pen in hand seems to release thoughts deep inside that I want to share with my Father. I may begin by giving Him thanks for the prayers He answered yesterday. As I begin to write to God, my Father, I usually realize where I am spiritually; as I write, it becomes more clear. When I'm confused or don't know where I am spiritually, I just begin to write, and eventually what is going on will surface.

I write about a sinful attitude or response that happened the day before. I write about something that is frustrating me or something I'm worried about. It helps to lay all these things before the Lord, even before I open my Bible, in order to hear His voice. But there is no right or wrong way to journal. It's simply about what helps you meet God.

For me, journaling primes my pump. Writing things down reinforces our ability to learn and remember. Record things God has just taught you; writing and reviewing His lessons helps keep the benefits fresh. Periodically, looking back at past learnings is a great source of confirmation and encouragement.

Fasting. Paul's first moments after encountering Jesus led him immediately into fasting and prayer (Acts 9:9,11). No one needed to teach him to do this; it was a reflexive response to divine revelation. Not long after, his missionary career was birthed out of ministering to the Lord in another time of fasting and prayer (Acts 13:2-3). Clearly, fasting was his modus operandi for connecting with the Spirit.

"A biblical definition of fasting is a Christian's voluntary abstinence from food for spiritual purposes" (*Spiritual Disciplines For the Christian Life* by Donald Whitney, p.160). Fasting from food diminishes the power of our physical energy and allows us to place a higher priority on our spirit. David confesses, "I humbled my soul with fasting" (Psalm 69:10).

Jesus did not command us to fast, but He assumed that after He departed His disciples would fast (Matthew 9:15). He wanted to make it crystal clear that no spiritual discipline—not fasting or any of these activities—earns favor with God (Matthew 6:16). The disciplines are simply pathways designed to feed our spirit. We use these to cultivate and nourish our fellowship with God.

Solitude and silence. Jesus, John the Baptist, many of the prophets, the desert fathers—all spent extensive time being alone. Dallas Willard believed that the reason Jesus spent time fasting in the desert was not to be at His weakest when facing Satan but to be at His strongest (*The Spirit of The Disciplines*, p.102).

Some leaders set aside one day each month to go away and be alone. My thousands of hours running and cycling alone have provided some of these benefits. I took one sabbatical of 70 days and spent many of the afternoons practicing silence and listening; it was a transformational experience for me.

Some activities are considered spiritual disciplines that don't seem like disciplines as much as just things that disciples do...things like witnessing, serving, tithing, celebrating, submitting, etc. Whatever you call them, they are modeled in scripture and enrich the life of a disciple. Finally, there are other spiritual disciplines that other leaders have written about and practiced with benefit: practices like frugality, secrecy, sacrifice, and simplicity. I can't speak to those directly, but the other practices discussed here have been absolutely foundational in my journey with the Father.

THE ART OF DISCIPLINE

Why would I call discipline an art?

There is frequently a general perception of discipline as "self-discipline": something we don't want to do but believe we should do. People who struggle with discipline often perceive the whole concept of discipline in this way and develop a very conflicted relationship with the activities that are designed to give us life.

Such efforts to "discipline ourselves" through this way of thinking has self-will as its source. So even when we succeed in this form of discipline, it only serves to strengthen the self-life...and that's contrary to the abiding that Christ offers us. At the same time we know that the right type of discipline is absolutely critical to success in any field of endeavor. So how does the type of discipline Paul envisions actually work?

Let's review the fundamentals. The ability to experience godly discipline comes from the Holy Spirit within us. It is a work of grace from start to finish, and like all sanctification it is a combination of God's work and ours cooperating together. So we do have a part to play.

The word "pleasure" in the Bible sometimes has a negative sense, and Christians often have the idea that pleasure is associated with sin. Yet Psalm 16:11 says, "In Your right hand are pleasures forever." Even God "takes pleasure in His people" (Psalm 149:4), and "it is God who is at work in you, both to will and to work for His good pleasure" (Philippians 2:13). The truth is that God is all about pleasure.

Sin promises pleasure but deceives us because it cannot give us the type of pleasure that is lasting and satisfying. What God intends for us to experience in discipline is trading lesser pleasures for higher ones. This is why I call it an art. I also think this is why Dallas Willard titled his book, *The Spirit of the Disciplines.*

We might choose to go to bed early so we can have time with God in the morning. Yes, this may involve some sacrifice when part of us wants to stay up late, yet when we make this trade, we experience more satisfaction and contentment with the results. Over time, this life-giving trade becomes habitual, even addictive. Others will look at this habit and only see self-discipline; we know differently.

I have run, cycled, and gone to the gym regularly for over 50 years. Some call it discipline and interpret it as an exceptional degree of willpower. It's not. It's just a trade. I consistently reap more benefits than the effort that goes into it, so I keep doing it. The same is true in regard to what I eat; I get more lasting pleasure from eating healthy foods than the all-too-quick-and-passing pleasure of eating sweet or fried foods. This is what I call "trading up": letting go of one thing to take hold of something infinitely more satisfying. I think Paul would agree.

DISCUSSION QUESTIONS

1. How easy do you find it to take Jesus up on His invitation to enter into His rest?

2. To what extent are you getting the daily spiritual resupply your soul craves?

3. How do you relate to the concept and the experience of discipline?

EIGHT

Tapping the Fuel
A Holy Spirit Invasion

In a previous chapter, we discussed the church and its vital role in carrying forward the ministry of Christ. Clearly, the early church was remarkable in the degree of miracles and extraordinary events that surrounded those first believers. Let's be honest—do we need the supernatural any less than they did? Have the challenges of life gotten any less potent in the last two thousand years?

Chapter 5 laid out the power that Jesus has made available to us so that sin shall not be our master any longer (Romans 6). That is foundational in our lives, but it's not the end of our need for power. Who needs wisdom today? Who needs healing for sickness? Who needs discernment of God's direction in life? Who needs the revelation of God's word and its practical applications in the workplace? All of us. Every single one of us.

Let's get more practical still.

Scenario 1. James has tremendous favor as a senior sales manager over the Atlantic states. Suddenly, he has a job offer to move across the country to the west coast; it comes with a substantial raise and recognition within the industry, yet his three teenagers are at a crucial place in their lives and community. What is God's best for James and his family?

Scenario 2. Lisa is a successful working mother, doing a good job juggling her role as a part-time nurse and full-time mom, yet her routine mammogram shows a small tumor in her breast and the biopsy is positive for cancer. What does God want to do in the lives of Lisa, her family, and the church in this fearful situation?

Scenario 3. Bill was laid off from his manufacturing job of 22 years in a declining industry that is fast becoming mechanized. Similar jobs currently on Monster.com are running at half the salary. After six months of futile searching, he's discouraged and depressed. How does God want to show up for Bill?

Scenario 4. Amy and John's oldest son is 15 and, after years of academic ease, he has just flunked a Physics class. He starts to call himself stupid and has lost interest in trying any more. Amy and John can't figure out whether their son needs psychological testing, a new school system, or a swift kick in the pants. The right decision could get their beloved son back on track; the wrong one could set him back at best and be destructive at worst. What is God up to?

When Jesus prayed over His disciples just before His death and ascension, He promised them a Helper, the "Spirit of truth" who "will guide you into all the truth" (John 16:7, 13). If guidance into truth was just about being a smart person, it wouldn't have required the supernatural invasion of the Holy Spirit. No, these real-world dilemmas call for divine intervention and provision, which is precisely why Jesus made the Holy Spirit available to us.

JESUS' DEPENDENCY UPON THE SPIRIT

Even Jesus did not venture into ministry without the anointing of the Spirit, so how could we think for a second that we could live the Christian life successfully without the same infilling?

Before Jesus begins to preach and heal, He counter-intuitively asks His cousin John to baptize Him in the river Jordan. When He comes up out of the water, the Holy Spirit descends upon Him looking something like a dove. Simultaneously, God speaks audibly to the crowd, affirming Jesus as His beloved Son and functionally ordaining Him for ministry in the power of the Spirit (Luke 3:21-22).

Remember that every prophet, priest, and king was anointed prior to serving in the Old Testament. In Luke 4:18, Jesus adopts the words of Isaiah declaring that "the Spirit of the Lord is upon Me"—a reference to His commissioning for ministry. When Pentecost occurs, we will see that anointing explode across all of God's people.

Let's look more carefully at how Christ Himself lived out his relationship with Father and in what way we can legitimately look to Him as our role model. Which brings us to a crucial question: *Did*

Jesus' miracles flow out of His divine nature or His human nature? In other words, was the supernatural a sign of Him being God or the natural extension of Him being a man? Theologically, we know that He was both—fully God and fully man. But we need to understand how this connects to the power He demonstrated.

This is important because if He performed miracles as God, then we can't expect to flow in that same power. If, however, He moved in supernatural authority as a man filled with the Holy Spirit, then we too can be filled with the Holy Spirit and do similar miracles.

Fortunately, Jesus answered this question directly in John 14:12. "He who believes in Me, the works that I do shall he do also; and greater works than these shall he do; because I go to the Father." Though it may feel daunting, that is great news!

What's more, Jesus adopted a reference to Himself that also speaks directly to His role as a Holy-Spirit-Anointed-Man; He calls Himself the "Son of Man" 90 times across the four gospels. Compare that to the 39 times He is referred to as the "Son of God." Of course, Jesus was fully both, but He seemed to anticipate our propensity to write off the supernatural caliber of His life as His god-ness rather than as normative for our own lives. It was the arrival of the Holy Spirit in earnest that flung wide open the door of our access to this life.

THE PENTECOST OFFER

Because Jesus went to the Father, the Holy Spirit has become the resident 24/7 Power Supply occupying the spirit of every believer! Pentecost was the first outpouring…and that flow has never stopped. Which leads to a pivotal question: *Is this baptism of the Holy Spirit still for us today, or was it a unique event specific to the early church?*

We know that for many decades much of the church has categorically repudiated the supernatural elements that characterized the first-century church. The theological word for this position is "cessationism," which refers to the spiritual gifts "ceasing" once scripture was written and recognized. The American evangelical church today operates primarily on the intellectual level and is more comfortable with studies in psychology than any talk about demons.

In spite of that, the Charismatic Renewal movement of the 60's and 70's brought a fresh induction of the Holy Spirit's role in producing a supernatural church. In fact a great number of today's aging leaders of many denominations were brought into the kingdom during this dynamic period.

So we might ask, *Where is the evangelical church today in terms of sponsoring "ordinary Christians" operating in the power of the Holy Spirit? Specifically the nine spiritual gifts listed by Paul in 1 Corinthians 12?* In my experience the evangelical church today is pretty quiet about any serious discussion of these issues. I think church leaders simply don't know how to integrate the spiritual gifts into the daily lives of their people. If I were to characterize Christians today, I don't think we would choose the word "supernatural." Perhaps the words "busy" or "trendy" are more appropriate.

But before we go any further, let's return to our question: *Is this supernatural power meant to be "normal" for the church today?* Conveniently, Peter answered this question quite directly in Acts 2:38-39. "Repent, and let each of you be baptized in the name of Jesus Christ for the forgiveness of sins; and you shall receive the gift of the Holy Spirit. For the promise is for you and your children, and for all who are far off, as many as the Lord our God shall call to Himself." In the context of Pentecost, this promise is not about salvation but about this spiritual outpouring described across the last couple chapters. With that sweeping declaration, Peter included every generation of Christ-followers in the Pentecost offer.

Now, let's look at the effects of this Spirit outpouring. Jesus had already connected the filling of the Holy Spirit to the power to witness (in Acts 1:8). And the effect was immediate. In response to Peter's Pentecost sermon, 3000 respond enthusiastically.

And in the remaining chapters of "The Acts of the Holy Spirit" it is clear that Pentecost was a continuing experience of the expanding church.

In Samaria, Philip preached with powerful, supernatural signs, and many believed the gospel and were baptized (Acts 8:5-12). Simon the magician, though rebuked by Peter for self-seeking motives, "saw" the Spirit being bestowed through the laying on of hands; evidently this was supernatural enough that Simon wanted to pay money to receive this ability (Act 8:9-19). And when Cornelius' household responded to the gospel, the Holy Spirit "fell upon all those who were listening to the message" with speaking in tongues (Acts 10:44).

Later in Ephesus, Paul asked the new disciples a question the evangelical church today would never ask: "Did you receive the Holy Spirit when you believed?" (Acts 19:2) They had not heard the whole gospel about Jesus, so when Paul shared with them, they responded and were water baptized (Acts 19:5). If we believe that Acts is the norm for our experience today, how unusual it is to us to find Paul laying his hands on these new converts that the Holy Spirit might "come on them" (Acts 19:6). "And they began speaking in tongues and prophesying." Clearly, this was a second experience with God.

UNWRAPPING THE GIFTS

The church Jesus birthed was a supernatural church, branded by the presence and power of the Holy Spirit. Remember, Jesus operated in the power of the Spirit, not because He was God but rather because He limited Himself to functioning as a Man (Philippians 2:6-8). And to extend his ministry, He then trained His disciples, sending them out to duplicate His ministry in the power of the Spirit (Luke 9 and 10).

On resurrection night He suddenly appeared behind closed doors and breathed upon His disciples, commanding them to receive the regenerating power of the Holy Spirit (John 20:22-23). Then He instructed them to wait for an anointing of Holy Spirit power that He called "the baptism of the Holy Spirit" (Acts 1:5), one purpose of which was to give His church power to witness throughout the world (Acts 1:8).

Let's turn our attention to the gifts themselves. What exactly did Jesus offer His church under this heading of spiritual gifts? It's easy to get confused at this point because scripture contains several lists of "gifts," including Romans 12:6-8 (sometimes called "motivational gifts") and Ephesians 4:11-12 (sometimes called the "five-fold gifts"). But the focus of our attention here is the list of nine gifts in 1 Corinthians 12:7-11, each a very supernatural expression specifically linked to the Holy Spirit. "To each one is given the manifestation of the Spirit for the common good."

The word of wisdom

This gift occurs when the Holy Spirit suddenly reveals a clear sense of what to do that provides a solution to an otherwise knotty problem. The classic Old Testament illustration of this gift is Solomon judging between two women who each claim to be the mother of a child. Since DNA-matching wasn't an option, Solomon moves in supernatural insight that did not come from intelligence but by the Spirit.

"Divide the living child in two, and give half to the one and half to the other," is his decree…a decision that one woman accepts and the other protests (1 Kings 3:16-28). Having flushed out the legitimate mother, Solomon gives the living child to the mother who protests, the one who clearly carries a mother's compassion.

The word of wisdom may come equally to you when you face a difficult situation. Rather than blundering on your impulses, you tune into *your spirit* and sense the divine leading of *the Spirit*. You wait, you listen, you depend. And the answer comes!

My son-in-law, Kendrick Vinar, is the senior pastor of Grace Church in Chapel Hill, NC, and he had long been funding a senior Cuban church planter without feeling a true sense of partnership. He called me one day, asking me what he should do. I listened and said, "Wow, you really need wisdom from God." He said, "Yeah, that's why I called you."

As soon as he said that, the Holy Spirit supernaturally dropped this thought into my mind. "Kendrick, you need to ask the senior leader to connect you with a young apostolic leader with whom you can form a relationship." As a result of this *word of wisdom*, a personal friendship and partnership was formed that has affected many Cubans in great ways.

Every disciple needs to rely upon the Holy Spirit to supply divine wisdom in everyday life situations. Think of all the times you need this in childrearing. Think of how the word of wisdom might operate in the business world. It is available!

The word of knowledge

The word of knowledge is a Holy-Spirit-inspired impression of some important piece of information or knowledge or insight that you would not otherwise know. This knowledge frequently acts like a key that unlocks a situation. It is the revelation of *data* rather than *application* (word of wisdom) that's in operation here.

This spiritual revelation can show up in different ways: suddenly knowing that someone needs you. An impression of a physical sickness or need. Sometimes it's a word of knowledge concerning what a person's role is within the body of Christ. My own sensitivity is uniquely tuned to those called to apostolic work; others are sensitive to other issues.

When the word of knowledge is given, it is usually accompanied with a sense of faith or confidence with respect to the knowledge. When I receive a word of knowledge about a person's illness, I normally have an unusual boldness in praying for that person to be healed.

When my son Jerome was thirteen, he was spending the night at a friend's house when I was awakened in the night. I had the distinct impression that he was calling me for help; in response, I prayed for him and went back to sleep. When I picked him up the next morning and mentioned it, he was visibly impacted. Apparently, he had experienced a high degree of inner torment and come very close to picking up the phone. God used that in a powerful way in his young soul.

Jesus moved in the word of knowledge all the time. Matthew 9:1-8 describes Him as perceiving the unspoken thoughts of the scribes, and Luke 6:6-11 reaffirms Jesus as "knowing what they were thinking in their heart." In John 4 Jesus told the Samaritan woman that she had been married five times and was living with yet another man.

The apostles also moved in the word of knowledge. Ananias was given knowledge to reach out to a recently-converted Paul (Acts 9:10-19). Philip received several words of knowledge regarding going to a certain place and approaching an Ethiopian's chariot (Acts 8:26-30). Clearly, Jesus intended his disciples to have access to supernatural knowledge.

The gift of faith

This gift is important to distinguish from "saving faith"—the faith that activates your relationship with God. In contrast, the spiritual gift of faith is a supernatural confidence in something that God plans to do.

Paul's vision to "come over to Macedonia and help us" was accompanied by an unusual gift of faith (Acts 16:9) that plays out over time. Even today, apostles operate in the gift of faith to break into new places and accomplish new things that do not seem humanly possible. Hudson Taylor's breakthrough into China in the mid-1800s was an example of apostolic faith.

Sometimes you might receive supernatural faith for a particular sum of money to use for a kingdom purpose. George Muller was given such a gift, leading an English orphanage to experience constant miracles of provision in that same time period. Many others have started various charities through the spiritual gift of faith.

Gifts of healing

There is a close link between the spiritual gifts of healing, faith, and miracles. One gift often bleeds over into the others, yet they can each also occur more singularly. Healing is a particular kind of miracle, and yet there are obviously miracles apart from healing. People often have a unique faith for particular types of healing—cancer, for instance, or infertility.

Jesus moved in all the spiritual gifts, and sometimes he linked specific healings to faith. Although faith is not mentioned directly when Jesus said to the man who had been ill for 38 years, "Get up, pick up your pallet and walk" (John 5:8), faith is implied. When the woman who had hemorrhaged for 12 years reached out to touch Jesus' garments, she exercised a very active faith (Mark 5:34).

Working of miracles

Miracles refer to unusual works of supernatural power that seem to violate natural laws. Raising the dead is perhaps the most compelling biblical example of this—an event rare in modern America but more commonplace in modern Africa and China.

116

Jesus raised two dead and regularly restored paralyzed limbs, withered hands, and blind eyes. Walking on water and calming a deadly storm were other expressions of Jesus living into the gift of miracles. Turning six jars of water into the finest wine is one of my personal favorites, each jar containing between 20 and 30 gallons (John 2)!

Paul raised a young man named Eutychus from the dead in Acts 20:9-10, and others were healed merely as Peter's shadow fell upon them (Acts 5:15). When Peter was wrongfully imprisoned in Acts 12:7-12, his chains supernaturally fell off, and he was led through doors opened by an invisible hand! I encourage all believers to cultivate an expectation toward the Holy Spirit to orchestrate out-of-the-box outcomes on a regular basis. This is simply the New Testament way to live.

Prophecy

I like to think of prophecy as the basic delivery system for Holy Spirit revelation. In that sense, a word of knowledge or a word of wisdom is "prophetic." The gift of prophecy may also be conceived of as an extended word of knowledge—a series of divine revelations about another person or situation. Prophecy can also be addressed to communities such as churches or cities or even nations.

1 Corinthians 14:3 tells us that the purpose of prophesy in the church should be for strengthening, encouraging, and comforting, which means that prophecy is not generally corrective in nature; this is a New Testament shift from much of what we see in books like Isaiah and Jeremiah. Along with that, New Testament prophecy is not typically a foretelling of future events as much as it is a "forth-telling" of God's heart in a given situation.

I believe this is the reason Paul uniquely spoke of prophecy as a gift we should all pursue (1 Corinthians 14:1)…because strengthening, encouraging, and comforting is so universal in its application. And prophecy uniquely accomplishes this. There is something about having a prophet "read our mail" and tell us things about ourselves only God could know that makes us feel deeply seen, affirmed, and loved. It activates faith toward whatever God is saying and doing in our lives.

Paul tells us that prophecy can be used to identify and impart spiritual gifts (1 Timothy 4:14; 1:18).

The discerning of spirits

This gift describes the ability given to a person by the Spirit to recognize a spirit or a spiritual dynamic in operation. It may be the discernment of whether another person is speaking or acting out of a divine or a demonic motivation.

In Acts 13:10 Paul identified a demon influencing Elymas the magician. Later in Acts 16:18 Paul identified a demon in a slave girl and commanded it to leave. In Acts 8:22-23 Peter discerned the spirit that was controlling Simon the magician.

Women are frequently very sensitive to spiritual forces, so I encourage husbands to listen carefully to their wives' perceptions. I like to think of my wife as having spiritual radar, and I take her warnings seriously, especially when it involves something sexual or occult. At the same time, a woman's sensitivity can sometimes make her a target of fear, calling for the husband-wife teamwork God designed.

Intercessors are often given discernment so that they may pray effectively. In Revelation 2:20 Jesus speaks to the church in Thyatira about not tolerating a woman whom He identifies as "Jezebel," probably a reference to the spirit behind the queen of Ahab in 1 Kings 16-21, a spirit of rebellion and deception associated with witchcraft. You can see why every Christian may at times need the ability to discern what spirit is at work in a situation or person.

Various gifts of tongues

The *gift of tongues* appears to be something different from the tongues spoken by those receiving the baptism of the Holy Spirit. This is not explicit in scripture, but we can deduce it from biblical references. Specifically, we see tongues having two different operations: one individual, one for the church. We have already seen that speaking in tongues is available to every believer as a "prayer language" from the believer to God which strengthens a person's inner life (1 Corinthians 14:14-15). In contrast *the gift of tongues* seems to be a prophetic message from God to His people. Speaking in tongues is a private conversation, while the gift of tongues is public...and thus requires interpretation.

The interpretation of tongues

The gift of tongues operates much the same as prophecy when it is interpreted. It is a message from God to the church (1 Corinthians 14:5), and its purpose is to build up the church (1 Corinthians 14:12). So Paul's requirement for the use of the gift of tongues in the public gathering is that it be interpreted for the understanding and application of all who hear it (1 Corinthians 14:13-28).

As you can see, Pentecost brought with it a whole array of supernatural tools for us to use in being the church. What if we were to experience these same gifts in the marketplace as much as within the church context? That's what we observe in the early church. And increasingly, we are beginning to return to that original strategy.

I believe that God's desire is for all His people to be filled with the Spirit and to operate in the supernatural in their day-to-day living. I fully expect the Holy Spirit to guide me and use me as I move about Gold's Gym. I regularly experience the gifts of healing, faith, wisdom, and the word of knowledge as I interact with unbelievers. I expect the Holy Spirit to speak to me or nudge me in regard to calling someone or changing my plans.

PURSUE THE GIFTS!

Author Sam Storms brings a valuable insight into understanding the nature of the spiritual gifts in his book, *The Beginner's Guide to Spiritual Gifts*.

> Spiritual gifts are not God bestowing to his people something external to himself. They are not tangible "stuff" or substance separable from God. Spiritual gifts are nothing less than God himself in us, energizing our souls, imparting revelation to our minds, infusing power in our wills, and working his sovereign and gracious purposes through us. Spiritual gifts must never

> be viewed deistically, as if a God "out there" has sent some "thing" to us "down here." Spiritual gifts are God present in, with, and through human thoughts, human deeds, human words, human love (p. 13).

The presence of the Holy Spirit in each one of us is simply a fulfillment of Jesus' incarnation purpose: *God with us* ("Immanuel," Matthew 1:23). You, being constantly filled with the Spirit, is the new normal you, and this is how every disciple can live.

I have heard pastors say, "I'm open to any gift God wants to give me," but they may not be asking, pursuing, expecting to receive the spiritual gifts. They may actively pursue gifts of leadership and teaching, but often they don't see why it's appropriate, desirable, and biblically necessary to be actively pursuing spiritual gifts. Yet this is clearly a command of God: "Pursue love, yet desire earnestly spiritual gifts" (1 Corinthians 14:1).

One way people receive spiritual gifts is through the laying on of hands. "Do not neglect the spiritual gift within you, which was bestowed on you through the laying on of hands by the presbytery. Take pains with these things; be absorbed in them, so that your progress will be evident to all" (1 Timothy 4:14-15). You can see how active Paul wants Timothy to be in pressing into God for the use of this gift. "Do not neglect" is strong language.

Paul continues to exhort his disciple: "For this reason I remind you to kindle afresh the gift of God which is in you through the laying on of my hands" (2 Timothy 1:6). Hebrews refers to the laying on of hands as one of the elementary teachings (Hebrews 6:1), but it isn't commonly used in today's church except in unusual situations.

Let's reach for more! If the Holy Spirit is offering us gifts, I for one want to unwrap the packages! The power of the Spirit is no less needed in today's world than it was in the Roman world, and the provision is no less available. Let's lay hands on one another and ask for every gift that the Spirit may want to bestow so that we can experience the same effectiveness today as we saw in the early church.

Before we close this chapter, let's take a quick look back at the real-world scenarios we raised at the opening. James is wrestling with the lure of a job raise but has concern over uprooting his three teenagers. What is God's best for him and his family? There is no direct scripture or biblical principle that neatly answers the nuances of this dilemma. But the Holy Spirit knows! What gift might the Spirit employ to reveal God's highest and best for this family? Perhaps a word of knowledge that God has good things for his family on the west coast. Perhaps a discerning of spirits that the new boss is untrustworthy. There is no substitute for timely revelation.

Lisa's biopsy comes back positive for breast cancer. What is God doing here? We have both scriptures for comfort and scriptures for healing—but what is the Spirit saying? Fear and suffering open us to the work of God like little else…so let's reach for the "now" word of God so that God's glory can be revealed and Lisa can walk with confidence into the future.

The other two scenarios speak the same message and invite us into the power of the Spirit. It doesn't mean there aren't legitimate times of pain and testing in the life of the Spirit; it does mean that the life of the Spirit is a supernatural life, and when we're operating in the gifts of God, we have the chance to *do life with* God in a whole new dimension.

DISCUSSION QUESTIONS

1. How has the presence and power of the Holy Spirit affected your life thus far?

2. Which spiritual gift (from Romans 12) seems most natural and evident in your life so far?

3. How do you feel God calling you to pursue the flow of the Spirit more intentionally in this season of your life?

NINE

Servant Leadership
Building a Healthy Marriage

Ours is a great love story. Nan's brother Frank took me to his home for a week of fun before entering the Air Force Academy together. Because his father was a Major General I, as a lowly cadet, could visit his home in nearby Colorado Springs. There to my surprise I discovered that he had a much younger sister, an amazing one at that. Today she is my Nan! I kissed this lady on my twenty-first birthday, and I was gone. Still am!

Cadets cannot be married according to school rules, but when Nan's father received orders for Brussels, Belgium, I knew I had to man-up and make a move. I asked the General for his daughter's hand, and when he agreed, we were secretly married at their home in Brussels. Upon graduation we were publically married in the cadet chapel with all the Air Force traditions. It was a great year.

We didn't know much about God's plan for marriage then, but we knew we were crazy about each other. Looking back, I would say we had at least a few principles working for us. We deeply loved and respected one another, she was big on communication, and we were both idealists. Plus, we were committed to doing life together. So when Nan became increasingly agitated over the realization that she did not know God, we took that journey together. It turns out that "doing life with" is huge in marriage as well as with Father God.

We learned all we could about following Jesus during my tours in and out of Vietnam and then in seminary. It didn't take long as a pastor and church planter to figure out that, in general, couples don't know much about respect and forgiveness, much less biblical roles. Very few husbands have been trained to become servant leaders, and so we became serious students of how to rescue troubled marriages and prepare young people before marriage.

In today's world blended families are often the norm. So we have to ask, did these men and women wake up one day and say to themselves, "I think I want my marriage to spiral down into arguments, misunderstandings, and mutual wounding. I'll let someone else raise my children while I give marriage another try with someone new. Maybe it'll work next time"? No, clearly people do not think this through.

Marriage doesn't have to be this way. We have walked with hundreds of couples into helping them discover God's secrets for lifetime happiness in marriage. It's far more about *being* the right person than *finding* the right person.

I'm not a country music fan, but this genre finds common cause in us all with our broken relationships, disappointments, and love lost. Now that I think about it, it's probably healthy to transform heartache into music. And the blues does that in spades. People need to keep hoping because the need doesn't go away just because of pain. Funny though, we don't hear much music that talks about the power of restoration.

Recently Dr. Clay Christenson of the Harvard Business School compared once-vibrant now-failed businesses with the failed marriages of his classmates. Since business is about the bottom line, the temptation is to invest in things that yield a profit immediately, whereas a competitor comes along and keeps improving a product—a strategy likely to pay off years later. We get that. Then he discussed how often his MBA classmates put all their energy into careers as opposed to the long-term payoff of wives and children. Twenty years later Dr. Christenson laments how many have their children being raised by someone else in another part of the country. It was a wakeup call to highly qualified professionals.

Family is a big deal for a reason; it's God's idea. He paints Himself as "the Father [of] every family in heaven and earth" (Ephesians 3:14-15). And the absolute core of family is the marriage—a concept so unique, so critical that our marital relationships are modeled after the Son of God and His Bride (Ephesians 5:23f). Little wonder then why Satan targeted the sacred relationship between a husband and wife as his first conquest (Genesis 3).

I had years of pilot training before anyone trusted me with an airplane solo. If that's the standard, you have to wonder how many years of training should be required for me to take another man's daughter and bring children into this world. Of course we could just say, "You look like a swell guy. I'll show you the control panel of my airplane, then hop in and take this beauty for a spin." That would explain the many burnt-over wrecks that litter the runway.

HEALTHY MARRIAGES BEGIN WITH A HEALTHY YOU

At the risk of oversimplification, there are two reasons marriages don't become the "happily ever after" that we naively expect when we say *I do*. Marriage takes two healthy people, and marriage takes a biblical plan.

Most people are not healthy in their own souls. We are born me-centered, insecure, independent, easily offended, not quick to forgive, and not accountable. Did I mention stubborn? Yet as God said to Adam, "It's not good for a man to be alone" (Genesis 2:18). God doesn't live alone, and He made us to need the benefits of loving relationships.

We need—even crave—love, affection, friendship, intimacy, being understood, loyalty. So now it starts to get interesting: we put two starry-eyed "in love" people together who do not know they are "me-centered" and find that their experience of love breaks down quickly.

God created marriage to satisfy our deepest needs, but it requires that two self-willed people become one (Genesis 2:24-25). One in vision, one in decisions, one in mutual care and concern. To be fair, Adam & Eve did not have our deficits; they were naked and not ashamed. Today, people don't seem to have much trouble with the naked part, but shame stalks us all. People are typically "packing" when it comes to things we want to hide.

Between years of pornography and before-this-marriage sexual experiences, people carry emotional wounds. Betrayals, rejections, angry words, disappointments—all these experiences produce shame, and shame attacks the core of our identity by obscuring the image of

God we are meant to portray. Many today come from divorced parents or abusive situations.

As I was writing this chapter, an email came from a dear friend of ours. Read it and see what you think.

Dear Nan,

Over the last 20 years I have had a ringside seat, observing several marriages: marriages that work, those that don't, those that end. As you know, my own marriage has had its ups and downs, all three of my daughters are divorced, one twice, and Julie's "union" also fell apart. And I have learned something. Our society, in church and out, has put an emphasis on "making marriage work." It's like asking two bad cooks to make a good dinner.

In our own case, two dysfunctional people loved each other, met certain of the other's needs and wanted a good marriage. Eventually Bob and I each met the Lord, and He healed us—still is actually and *then* the marriage started working. Almost of its own accord.

My daughters are dysfunctional—how I want that to not be true, but it is. Lucy is married. She and her husband get along, meet certain of each other's needs, but she says they are not well connected. I see hurt people trying to have a healthy marriage.

I have friends, both of whom so want the "dinner" of a good marriage. One of them has submitted to the Lord for healing and become a good & healthier "cook." One wants to receive the good dinner, wants to be healthy and happy, but will not submit to the Lord for the cure.

I think of you. Married to the love of your life at 16, then realizing that it was not enough. You and your husband each totally gave yourselves to God, not to achieve a good marriage, but to become godly, healed individuals. And, of course, God answered, pushed down and overflowing, healthy lives, a wonderful marriage. Grateful for you, Janice.

God designed marriage to reveal where we are in our emotional, spiritual, relational health. Which works well if God is your friend, and you have the relationship to learn from Him and draw from Him. Often in church we receive good teaching, but if we aren't healthy as people, chances are good that the marriage will fail to satisfy. The best thing you can bring to a marriage is a healthy you.

PURSUING A HEALTHY SOUL

If you're single (or single again), your job is to become a healthy person. Use your time to become emotionally and spiritually healthy instead of just trying to find the "right" person. As you become healthy, you will become more alert to signs that indicate lack of health in others...which will help you not marry an unhealthy person. A person's wellness of soul can often be detected by others who are older and mature.

How can we become increasingly healthy in our souls? No one can do this for you but you. You can't control what others do to you, but you have to take responsibility for your own actions. We do not come from a level playing field; some have been subjected to much more violence and injustice than others. Very true. Still, the path to health involves taking ownership for your choices now.

Are you living on a performance basis, meaning that you only receive God's love when you are measuring up? This will cripple your soul. Your spiritual and emotional health come from receiving Father's love and actively living in it. This is the journey of people who are getting healthy.

I think of two sons, one is eight and the other is nine. Both are chosen last on their two teams; both were later bullied, snubbed, and called names. One came home and crawled into Dad's lap, telling him all about it. Dad listened, held him, rocked him, spent time with him, whispered in his ear...and he jumped off a happy boy. The other son held it all inside and refused to sit in Dad's lap. Which one was becoming healthy? Which one are you?

Jesus came to lead us into Father's Lap. Every morning I've got to have some "Lap-time." I'll never be better than the amount of Father's love, reassurance, forgiveness, acceptance, life, and joy that I actually receive. This is where health begins.

Health continues with how we handle the inevitable conflicts, hurts, and offenses that life brings us—but we will look at that more in the next chapter. Suffice it to say that you will block your own experience of God's forgiveness if you do not learn the art of forgiving others.

Ephesians 4:26-27 says, "Be angry, and yet do not sin; do not let the sun go down on your anger, and do not give the devil a place." This is Rule #1 in marriage. If you are willing to go to sleep with anger and unforgiveness in your soul, this one sin will eat your lunch. You give the devil permission to rob you of peace, joy, and emotional well-being.

So let's learn this skill first as we begin to look at other marriage skills.

A BIBLICAL PICTURE

Assuming that we have all suffered some pain in marriage and that we are all now seeking to become healthy in our own souls, let's turn our attention toward the tools for a solid, healthy marriage. Most of us who are married today look back and think, *I didn't know anything about creating and maintaining a healthy relationship.* What we now know is that it really comes down to character.

To be blunt: marriage issues are character issues. And we all have character problems. The gospel is God's power to set us free from all the ways we are not like Christ. If you are living in the gospel, you are on the path to becoming a healthy person. So let's get practical.

Here is where I begin with every man I mentor: *I'm not your wife's pastor; you are.* My job is to help husbands learn to do a good job in this essential role. Probably 99% of men were not taught how to do this, but you can learn.

Adam handed us men the worst possible model: a passive husband. The first rule of leadership is *Show Up*. It takes courage to be a good husband because you are now responsible for things for which you do not feel equipped. When we men feel insecure, we have a tendency to hide: playing golf, going fishing, getting under a car, or just going back to work. These make for great activities but poor mistresses.

Wives, when your husband shows up, what is your attitude? God says your first role is to be his helper (Genesis 2:18). A "helper suitable for him" means that you will want to be teachable, learning how and what helps him succeed in his role as servant-leader.

Remember that God, the Holy Spirit, is Himself called "The Helper" (John 14:16) so this is a very important, holy role.

The Godhead has roles too. The Father, Son, and Holy Spirit are all equal, but they don't have the same function. They don't compete with one another; they complement one another as described in 1 Corinthians 11. Likewise, scripture is very clear that men and women are both created in God's image (Genesis 1:27). Both are equal in value and worth. But if we don't get the roles right, the relationship will not yield God's plan for our oneness.

My wife is a lot smarter than I am, but this thrills me! Why? Because she loves being my helper. She is totally secure in her worth and her role. She doesn't want to be the final decision-maker in our home. She wants full access and input, and I want that also for a very practical reason: I need her wisdom. She has studied me and knows how to speak in ways that help me see blind spots without being my mother. She believes in me.

UNTANGLING THE SUBMISSION KNOT

Submission can be a knotty issue for couples and is frequently misunderstood and misapplied. Submission begins with the mutuality of Ephesians 5:21. I am the leader, and yet I submit to my wife, meaning that I respect her insights, her feelings, and her needs. I make it a priority to listen to her. It is my pleasure to honor her as Peter describes (1 Peter 3:7). And yet, within all of it, I am to listen carefully for Father's voice.

Within this context of honest sharing and respect, my wife wants me to make the final decision and doesn't try to intimidate me to do her will. She trusts me. God's guidelines for marriage roles are simple and are spelled out in Ephesians 5:22-23. The two of us are to function as one. Somebody has to be the leader, and that responsibility goes to the husband.

God will hold the husband primarily accountable for the well-being of his wife and the relationship. Husbands, if you show up and listen for God's voice, He will give you wisdom that comes from Him. This is where James 1:2-5 comes into play: *Ask for the wisdom you need!*

Here's a quick example. I led a man to Christ who eventually became a pastor; unfortunately, he is now separated from his wife. His overbearing, harsh treatment of the entire family required her honest feedback. It was years of passive enabling before she began to offer that feedback. Misunderstanding how submission was to be lived out, she did not feel the freedom to share her genuine thoughts and feelings with him until it was too late. Honest communication between husbands and wives is essential to the unity and oneness God envisions.

Whose fault is this? Both, but God will start with the husband. He was not the servant leader who made his wife feel safe to speak up. He used his anger as a weapon. Let's take a fresh look at the blueprint in Ephesians 5.

Men, if you are not experiencing Christ nourishing and cherishing you, you will feel unprepared to nourish and cherish your wife. Especially when there are problems.

If you are trying to measure up and become adequate in yourself, you will fail, and you'll live like an insecure man, trying to hide it by being either passive or macho.

Men, we must learn to use our weaknesses (2 Corinthians 12:9-10). We should come to Jesus needy every day. Because He loves us, He does not condemn us, and we don't have to hide or pretend. My many weaknesses become channels for drawing on God's power and help. Maybe we should pray Paul's Ephesians 3 prayer every morning:

> For this reason I bow my knees before the Father, from whom every family in heaven and on earth derives its name, that He would grant you, according to the riches of His glory, to be

strengthened with power through His Spirit in the inner man, so that Christ may dwell in your hearts through faith; and that you, being rooted and grounded in love, may be able to comprehend with all the saints what is the breadth and length and height and depth, and to know the love of Christ which surpasses knowledge, that you may be filled up to all the fullness of God (verses 14-19).

Scripture paints a picture of husbands treating wives just like Christ treats His Bride. And as a general rule, when I look at your wife, I see what it's like to live with you 24/7. When a wife thrives and emanates joy, it is clear that she is well-loved and cared for. And vice versa. When I married Nan, I could see what it was like for her to live under her father's care and leadership, which had been done well.

I am to be the servant leader of my wife, and she is my first responsibility. Before God will ask me about church or business, He will ask me about my wife. So my job is to be Christ-like: to feed her emotionally and spiritually so that she is her best self (Ephesians 5:26-27)! In order to do that well, I need to be in constant touch with what is going on inside her...and this happens for us each morning with an hour of journaling, absorbing Scripture, sharing, and praying together.

RULES OF ENGAGEMENT

A young man who had been married a month asked me, "What one piece of advice do you have for a young man just married?" I said, "Watch the drift."

I'm now mentoring a very godly young man with a great marriage who just realized that he was drifting. He's busy, she's busy. They have two young children, and he started a construction company. Now he has started a media company as well. The drift comes subtly and unintentionally. The key is to catch it early and reverse that flow with intentionality and servant leadership.

Even better, be proactive in forging your oneness so that the drift can't get off the ground. Part of this relational stewardship includes clears boundaries in communication, much like what the military calls "rules of engagement." Here's an essential "No no" list:

- No shouting.

- No screaming.

- No slamming doors, cabinets, or throwing things.

- No name-calling.

- No cursing.

- No conversations that begin with, "You always..." or "You never...."

- No physical force of any kind.

- No sharing your marriage issues with family or friends; this only happens with a professional, confidential counselor.

- In the heat of your emotions do not exaggerate or say things in a provocative way.

- Never refer to your mate as "my old lady" or "my old man."

- Never look at other women in the way that men do. You may be attracted visually, but do not linger there or express desire for someone else.

- Never compare your mate to another man or woman.

- Never say, "I married the wrong person. I was warned, etc."

- Never threaten divorce as a tool of manipulation.

- Never engage in pornography. This is death to a relationship! If this is an issue, get deliverance immediately with a trusted spiritual leader.

Now that we're clear on what *not* to do in a marriage relationship, let's look at what will actively build a healthy union:

- Always make it your business to be a "one-woman man" and a "one-man woman."

- Treat your wife like a lady and your husband like a gentleman; people usually live up to your expectations.

- Use your manners at home. Keep yourself groomed and attractive for your mate.

- Practice self-control and respectful communication. Every person has some sensitive hot buttons, and we want to be able to communicate in a way that is clear but keeps the other from feeling insulted or disrespected.

- Live graciously with your mate. Believe the best. Let small offenses pass.

- Really listen to your mate and try to understand where the real hurt is coming from. Use conflict as a way to learn rather than defend yourself.

- Make it your mutual aim to forgive one another and pray over the difficulty before going to sleep (Ephesians 4:26-27).

- Be the first one to see your part in causing an offense; then humble yourself and ask for forgiveness. The first one to the cross is the leader.

- If there is a serious offense, try to find out where the hurt comes from. Many of us come into marriage carrying previous wounds that make it hard for us to respond in a mature, loving way.

- Honor your spouse in casual conversation in front of your children or anyone else.

- Thank your mate every day for almost everything he or she does. In other words, don't take the service of one another for granted.

Study the God-given differences between men and women. I love the book title, *Men Are Like Waffles; Women Are Like Spaghetti* by Bill & Pam Farrel. We men tend to compartmentalize, whereas for women everything is connected. Men can have twenty things going on and go to sleep; we often have the capacity to focus and ignore other important issues ("waffles"). Women, on the other hand, can change topics instantaneously ("spaghetti") because "this" reminds her of "that," and she can assume that you are following when, in fact, you are totally lost.

I like to say, "A man's memory about relational things tends to be like a trash can, whereas a woman's memory about your relationship is like a hard drive." She will remember everything you ever said to her that blessed her or hurt her. So treat her carefully. Men, study your wife and make it your joy to understand her. She is unique, and she is the one God gave you. Do all you can to enhance her life, and you will be the recipient of a grateful wife.

THE TEN-COW WIFE

There is an old story from Reader's Digest that takes place on an island in the Pacific. In this culture it was common for men to offer one, two, or (on rare occasion) three cows to a prospective father-in-law for his daughter in marriage.

One young woman in the village was rather ordinary, and her father never expected more than a single cow for her when that day came. So the village was stunned when a wealthy young man offered the father *ten cows* for her hand in marriage.

People just couldn't understand this profound act. Was it the lavishness of the rich, the exuberance of youth, or just the foolishness of the ignorant? When asked, this young man had a single reply, "I wanted a 10-cow wife." He wanted the best—and received it. Years later a reporter was in this man's home and heard the story. He reported first-hand what a regal woman this man's wife was. In other words, she became the way she was treated and valued by her husband.

This point hits close to home for me. My mother died at age 73, and a few years later Dad remarried a woman with whom he was not very compatible. Eventually he wanted to separate, but as his kids we urged him to reconsider. I gave him a work list derived from *The Five Love Languages*. In this excellent book author Gary Chapman pitches the idea that love needs to be expressed in five ways, or "languages," in a healthy marriage.

So I challenged my father to practice the following with his wife every day:

- *Physical touch*: to convey love by touching her at least twice a day. Touch her face, her arm in some way that conveys affection.

- *Quality time*: to spend at least an hour a day listening to her, looking into her eyes. Find out what she is experiencing in her life each day.

- *Serving*: to do something practical for her daily. Begin to develop the habit of serving her in ways she doesn't expect.

- *Words of affirmation*: to observe her and look for all the ways you can genuinely notice and appreciate positive things about her. And then put them into words!

- *Gift giving*: to give her a gift every week that is not practical. Something more personal or romantic.

At the end of two months I asked Dad how things were going. He said, "She's doing much better." I just smiled.

So how will your story be written? What will your children and grandchildren tell their friends and their children about your marriage? What will God have to say about the priority you placed on this most precious of relationships?

Even if your marriage has experienced damage, it can be restored by living in the truths and practicing the tools offered here. If you have never been married, you have a new set of skills to bring to that relationship. And if you're starting over from past failure, today is the day to make it count and to build a heritage for the future.

DISCUSSION QUESTIONS

1. How challenging do you find it to be a humble servant in your marriage?

2. With as much honest objectivity as possible, how healthy are you as an individual…and how does that affect your marriage?

3. How well do you and your spouse do with the "Rules of Engagement"?

4. How can you improve your "fluency" in the five love languages this month?

TEN

Kingdom Authority
Aligning Your Relationships for Blessing

I was probably thirteen, riding in the car with my father, when he ran a stop sign. Not by accident. I could tell that he saw the sign and blew right through it, on purpose. In typical thirteen-year-old omniscience, I called him on it. But I was caught off guard by his response: "Son, these rules are for ordinary people." Wow. I got the message loud and clear—as non-ordinary people, we got to choose which rules we would obey and which ones we wouldn't.

I took Dad's advice to heart not long afterwards by "borrowing" the family car (still thirteen) and driving it around town with my buddies while my father was away on business. I managed to pull off the entire adventure without mishap…but we lived in a small southern town where there were no secrets. I had been seen! And when a business owner downtown called my father to tell on me, he got a tongue-lashing in return. I got nothing. Apparently Dad was proud of my industrious rule-breaking and never mentioned it.

Six years later I entered the Air Force Academy, and boy was I in for a rude awakening.

For the entire first year of the program, we cadets were subjected to the constant high-octane grillings that are the stuff of movies. No matter what the circumstances, no matter how justified our behavior, there was only one acceptable answer to any challenge: "No excuse sir!" Only one. Any attempt to explain was like the scent of blood to a pack of sharks. This naïve cadet quickly learned that submission to authority was the only lesson in play that year.

The military was a unique tool in the hands of God for my life. In that moment of decision, my "No excuse sir" broke the iron vein of independence that had been cultivated all my childhood. I wasn't really rebellious; I simply craved adventure and had gone after it in typical Type-A fashion. But that was now over and done. From then on, I was ready to learn.

The military is structured to operate well in a high-stress environment. To be led by men who are under authority where accountability leads to trust—something not possible when every man does what is right in his own eyes. Our culture, however, is missing this chip. The proper use of and value for authority are not topics of discussion, whereas any case of its abuse shows up on the front page news.

Everyone has stories about the wrong use of authority. Our bad experiences with a parent, a teacher, a boss, a policeman, or the government confirm the biblical account. According to scripture, the world left the rule of the Good Authority only to come under a Not Good Authority, namely the devil. He's known as "the god of this world." Everyone knows something is dreadfully wrong with our world, yet few connect their experience with the issue of authority.

The biblical view of our world includes a spiritual dimension filled with realities beyond human sight. Angels, demons, rulers of this unseen world, the Holy Spirit—not to mention our own inner spirit—all interact behind the scenes to produce what we observe with our eyes. In this unseen realm, spiritual authority is the determining factor.

For Westerners the account of Jesus' encounter with Satan must challenge their most basic presuppositions. I suspect it's like an American coming into a cricket match at half time. The devil is tempting Jesus, making promises to Him. These were the forty days that changed the world. This was the tipping point, and it was all about authority.

My appeal to skeptical Americans is this: Since we know something is dreadfully wrong with this world, something no one seems able to explain, why not entertain the possibility that God is offering to take us behind the curtain? Let's start by asking a great question, *Why did Jesus initiate a confrontation with the devil before He announce the Kingdom of God, cast out demons, or healed?* The answer? Authority.

Satan had not encountered a single person in all history—not one—that he could not tempt to sin and thus gain legal authority over him. By not sinning, not submitting to the devil, Jesus emerged from His forty-day test having "bound the strong man" (Matthew 12:29). This set the stage for Jesus' spiritual coup of reclaiming rightful rule over planet earth, the entrance of the kingdom of God.

RESTORING A CULTURE OF AUTHORITY

Every culture has some things that reflect God's counter-culture and some things that reject God's ways. For example, many oriental societies honor the aged whereas our culture dishonors them. Some cultures do not have a word for conscience, and you can imagine the consequences of that culture gap.

In African and Latin societies family is everything, whereas in our culture everything is about the individual. Asian cultures generally overlook the individual for the sake of the larger community; they have an emphasis on honor that is foreign to us.

Americans spend billions of dollars every year on dogs and cats—absolutely incomprehensible to most cultures around the world that have no grid for animals outside of food and farm use.

Growing up in a culture means that we usually accept its dominant worldview, norms, and assumptions without ever being conscious of it. It is simply the way life is. Unchallenged and unevaluated. As we study Scripture and examine our own society we want to increasingly discern how American assumptions differ from God's, and specifically we want to inspect our ideas related to authority.

Americans are fiercely independent due to our history; the very formation of our nation came out of rebellion to the tyranny we experienced under another country's rule. This independent spirit is fiercely suspicious of authority; the greater the power wielded by a person, the more we tend to question its legitimacy.

We are much more comfortable speaking of influence, not authority. And as a leader, I would rather rely upon my influence than authority, but the danger is that we don't teach the proper God-given role of authority. Fulfilling our destinies requires that we live under authority so as to properly use our authority.

American Christians forfeit many of God's choice blessings because they make decisions independently, without regard for their authorities...and feel justified in disrespecting the authorities God places over their lives. They do not understand that by doing this they give the devil the right to exercise his authority over them—which we'll explore more in a minute.

John 1:11-12 says, "He came to His own, and His own did not receive Him. But as many as received Him, to them He gave the right to become children of God." John Bevere shares a powerful truth concerning the two groups described in this verse: "Many times God will send us what we need in a package we don't want. This very presentation will manifest the true condition of our heart, exposing whether we are submitted to His authority or resistant to it" (*Under Cover*, by John Bevere, p. 121).

I find that newer generations of Christians seem most likely to think it's their right to judge God's opinions. For this reason, many hold opinions about life, values, and relationships that differ from Scripture. Few think in terms of the government, the boss, the law, the leader, or the husband as being God's delegated authority.

OBEDIENCE IN RESPONSE TO GOD'S AUTHORITY

Any time we encounter authority we are dealing with God. God created us in His image and stated our destiny in the most amazing terms: Be fruitful, multiply, fill, subdue, and rule (Genesis 1:27-28). However, the effectiveness of our mandate depended upon our operating under God's authority. God made man to be His viceroy—to both be under His authority and to rule with authority.

God set the boundaries for man so that Adam would learn obedience, the very definition of being under authority (Genesis 2:16-17). Eve came out from under the authority of her husband by disobeying him (Genesis 3:6). And Adam came out from under God's authority by joining her in disobedience. At the center of it all was their determination to decide good from evil, a role that belonged to God, not them.

One definition of evil is precisely what happened in the garden: to reject what God says. To resist God's authority. Satan is the architect of such a posture and built his kingdom, his spiritual realm upon this rebellion against God's authority (Isaiah 14:12-17; Ezekiel 28:12-17). Ultimately there are only two authorities in this world: God and Satan. And we will choose one.

The sad denigration of man and the earth is the result of Adam coming out from under authority and protection. Jesus came as the "new Adam" who remained under God's authority—with the result that He had authority over Satan. He didn't choose the cross; he chose obedience, which took Him to the cross.

This is why Jesus stated in Matthew 7:21 that doing God's will (or remaining under God's authority) is the test of salvation. Notice that it's not a matter of what we do for God but our obedience that is the crux. In order to be under God's authority and free from Satan's, we must give up deciding for ourselves what is good or evil. This belongs to God.

OBEDIENCE TO HUMAN AUTHORITIES

Thus the whole idea that we might preach the gospel and not remain under the human authorities God places over our lives is to operate within the realm of Satan's error. I realize this is a foreign language to most of us. It is not on our screens or in our equations for understanding life.

When Paul met Christ, he recognized His authority and called Him "Lord," submitting himself to his rule (Acts 9). Paul then respected the very bad authorities who challenged his divine call: both the Roman government and the high priest, writing, "Every person is to be in subjection to the governing authorities. For there is no authority except from God, and those which exist are established by God. Therefore whoever resists authority has opposed the ordinance of God; and they who have opposed will receive condemnation upon themselves" (Romans 13:1-2).

With these issues in mind, you can see why Scripture says it's so important to teach our children to both honor and obey their parents.

The reason given: "So that it may be well with you, and that you may live long on the earth" (Ephesians 6:1-3). That is some good fruit from the practice of obedience.

Later in Acts 23:2-5 Paul describes his submission to even the Jewish authority of his day.

> The high priest Ananias commanded those standing beside him to strike him on the mouth. Then Paul said to him, "God is going to strike you, you white-washed wall! Do you sit to try me according to the law, and in violation of the Law order me to be struck?" But the bystanders said, "Do you revile God's high priest?" And Paul said, "I was not aware, brethren, that he was high priest; for it is written, 'You shall not speak evil of a ruler of your people.'"

Paul understood how our disobedience gives Satan the right to exercise his authority over us. In Ephesians 4:25-32 Paul seems to relate lying, ongoing anger, stealing, and bad words with two things: giving the devil a "place" (an authority, a right) in our lives, and grieving the Holy Spirit of God.

Satan is not afraid of us when we violate an authority over our lives, whether it be governmental authority, organizational authority, marriage authority, or church authority. We have given away our own spiritual authority in that moment and ceased to be a threat to him.

Of course, this raises an immediate and important question: What are we to do when we are under a bad or evil authority? Biblically, we have a number of legitimate options.

We can make an appeal to authority as Daniel did in Daniel 1:8, where he requested permission to forego the royal food in favor of kosher fare. Alternatively, we can refuse an evil authority as Peter and John did in Acts 4:19-20 as long as, like them, we are willing to suffer the consequences. They respectfully refused to obey man because they were under specific orders from God. They weren't rebellious; they simply had to make a choice between a greater and lesser authority. If they were to die, then they would die.

Fundamentally, we must not obey an authority that requires us to disobey God's word. If a husband demands that his wife stop worshipping God or commit an immoral act, he must be disobeyed. If a husband is physically abusive to his wife or children, she may separate "bed and board." Daniel's friends who faced the fiery furnace are good examples of this (Daniel 3). David had to flee his authority because Saul was dangerous; even so, David kept a humble and respectful attitude.

So there are some practical steps that Christians can take in situations of abusive authority that do not compromise the biblical imperative of submission. Let's look at more examples of right alignment with human authority that yielded spiritual authority in the lives of Gods' people.

EXAMPLES OF RIGHT ALIGNMENT

Jesus. As usual, our best example comes from Jesus. Hebrews 5:8-9 says that "although He was a Son, He learned obedience from the things which He suffered. And having been made perfect, He became to all those who obey Him the source of eternal salvation." In other words, Jesus took the role of the "second Adam" and remained under Father's authority on our behalf. He did not function apart from full reliance upon His Father. Never did He act on His own initiative.

Obedience out of relationship with God is how the kingdom of God functions. Watchman Nee points out that Jesus did not feel obligated to answer Pilate's interrogations because "He was not under earthly jurisdiction. But when the high priest adjured Him by the living God, then He replied. This is obedience to authority" (p.15).

David. One of the great secrets to King David's friendship with God and his success in so many ways was his respect for the bad authority placed over him. King Saul tried his utmost to track David down and kill him for many years. And remember, David had already been anointed king! If anyone had a right to attack his evil authority, it was him. Yet David refused to kill Saul when he twice had the chance.

When his men did not understand his forbearance, David replied, "Far be it from me because of the Lord that I should do this thing to my lord, the Lord's anointed, to stretch out my hand against him, since he is the Lord's anointed" (1 Samuel 24:6). Saul on the other hand lost his kingdom because he disobeyed God's orders, making his own decision about what was right and wrong despite clear orders from God (1 Samuel 15:9).

Saul's partial obedience cost him his kingdom and destiny for himself and his sons. The prophet Samuel's response was classic: "Has the Lord as much delight in burnt offerings and sacrifices as in obeying the voice of the Lord? Behold, to obey is better than sacrifice.... For rebellion is as the sin of divination, and insubordination is as iniquity and idolatry. Because you have rejected the word of the Lord, He has also rejected you from being king" (1 Samuel 15:22-23).

The Centurion. It's interesting to me that the one example of a man who recognized Jesus' authority was a military man. The centurion said, "Lord, I am not worthy for You to come under my roof, but just say the word, and my servant will be healed. For I also am a man under authority, with soldiers under me; and I say to this one, 'Go!' and he goes, and to another, 'Come!' and he comes, and to my slave, 'Do this!' and he does it."

"Now when Jesus heard this, He marveled and said to those who were following, 'Truly I say to you, I have not found such faith with anyone in Israel'" (Matthew 8:8-9). Jesus called this recognition of authority "faith." The key to this centurion's understanding was this: being under authority gave him the right to exercise authority.

In the military, a captain only has authority down-line because he is under authority. In the kingdom, God backs up those who submit to His authority wherever their authority is needed.

John Bevere tells how God taught him an important lesson when he was resisting the authority in his life. Working as a youth pastor in a large church for eight months, he had been creating Friday night "parties" for teens, with his pastor's blessing. In a staff meeting, the pastor unexpectedly told everyone that the Holy Spirit had given him orders to not have small groups.

John was horrified and said, "You don't mean the youth, pastor?" Four times the senior pastor repeated the Holy Spirit's orders to a bewildered, devastated youth pastor. John was positive that he was right and that the senior pastor wrong! He saw it as the senior pastor canceling the salvation of hundreds of teens, and he was hot!

Going home he poured out his complaints to his wife, but was shocked to hear her say, "Well, it looks like God is trying to teach you something." John was staring out the window when the Holy Spirit finally spoke to him. "John, whose ministry are you building? Mine or yours?" *Yours, Lord!* was his instant reply. The Holy Spirit said, "No, you're not! You're building your own. John, when I brought you to this church to serve this man, I made you an extension of the ministry I entrusted to him. I called you to be his arms and legs; I put only one man in charge of a ministry" (*Under Cover*, by John Bevere, p.17).

From this crisis God began to teach John what would become an enduring life-lesson. Suddenly he was able to observe the many ways godly men in the Bible modeled living under authority. I appreciate John sharing his personal journey in learning this biblical truth.

PRACTICAL APPLICATIONS OF AUTHORITY

So our work is cut out for us in this department—first in our own hearts and second in the lives of those we lead. In making disciples, we need to teach people to recognize and obey authority. Here are a few simple ways we can do it:

1. We first accomplish this by defining salvation in terms of coming under (and remaining under) God's authority.

2. Next, we train them to respond to human authority with obedience as unto God.

3. Then we teach them to use their authority as a way to serve God by serving others.

4. Perhaps the most potent practical application of right alignment with authority comes in the area of forgiveness.

THE ALIGNMENT OF FORGIVENESS

When our children were young, they had a story record that spun colorful accounts of speaking animals who taught vital life lessons. One of the stories I've never forgotten—partly because the voices were so annoying and partly because the truth is so enduring!

Stewart the money lived in a cage at the zoo, and one day the zookeeper accidentally dropped the key to his cage within arm's reach. The clever monkey waited until the keeper's back was turned before he reached out his arm and snatched up the key. Gleeful with anticipation, he waited for night to fall before unlocking his door and stepping outside into sweet freedom.

"I'm free, I'm free," Stewart sang as he danced around the outside of his cage and flaunted his prowess to the other nearby animals. Before he scampered away, however, he spied a banana sitting on the floor of his cage and figured it would be good to take a snack as he made good on his escape.

Sticking his arm back through the bars of the cage, he seized the banana...only to find that his fist could no longer squeeze back through the bars as long as he held the banana. Irritated, he pulled harder. His joy turned to frustration, which gave way to downright rage as he strained stubbornly to take what was rightfully his.

You can see where the story is going. The zookeeper returns the next morning to find Stewart wrestling vainly and furiously, having sacrificed his liberty all for the sake of a lone banana. It was his by rights, and he refused to let go. A compelling metaphor for the bondage of unforgiveness.

It's just so blooming unfair!

Everything within us rises up in outcry against the act of releasing another person's wrong-doing. Forgiveness appears as foolishness...even when we know we should. We know the drill: we get wronged and hurt by another person, only to nurse the offense, replaying the situation over and over in our heads. Resentment settles in, and eventually bitterness sets up shop.

Now that we've invested so much energy in the rightness of our cause, the idea of releasing such a person feels ludicrous. Cynicism now begins to color our view of others as trust recedes and we anticipate being wronged yet again. This spiritual cancer has generated an enormous degree of suffering among humans, both Christians and unbelievers alike. But not only does unforgiveness cause us pain, it erodes our authority by making room for our spiritual enemy.

BREAKING THE ENEMY'S AUTHORITY

Remember Ephesians 4:26-27 from last chapter? "Be angry, and yet do not sin; do not let the sun go down on your anger, and do not give the devil a place." This is not just for married couples; this pervasive truth speaks to every human relationship. So every time we justify and retain our anger, we do indeed invite the devil to exercise his destructive authority over our lives and undermine God's authority over us.

Anger is a powerful force, and while Paul differentiates between anger and sin, it's a slippery slope to be sure. In Matthew 5:22, Jesus says that "everyone who is angry with his brother shall be guilty before the court." When our wills are crossed, anger is the typical result, which is why Paul says, "When you're angry, don't let it make you sin!" Don't let it hang around, not even for a day.

I suspect that most of us have generational curses that involve unforgiveness and anger—places where we feel justified in holding onto memories and feelings of offense. We can spot them when we catch ourselves reacting disproportionately to a situation. The depth of emotion betrays the presence of a malignant undercurrent, an abiding presence of hostility lurking just beneath the surface of our awareness.

Even when we are absolutely right, we are being controlled by the object of our unforgiveness rather than by God! Technically speaking, that's idolatry. Practically speaking, it's slavery.

Let's imagine that you were sexually abused...or racially rejected...or even bullied violently. When you see that dynamic in play with someone else, your blood begins to boil. It's a grievous wrong and immense injustice—and it's been part of your own historical pain. Yet unforgiveness allows that pain to remain and fester, while releasing the abuser (not from earthly accountability but

147

1

from your judgment) allows you the chance to go free. Like Stewart the monkey.

God is committed to our freedom. This is precisely why He has established the law of forgiveness. If you want to be free, you must forgive those who have hurt you. Period. No wiggle room. His deal is this: *If I forgive you, you have to forgive them* (Matthew 6:12; 18:32-34).

When we don't release people from what they "owe" us, it blocks our ability to receive from God. It blocks our ability to follow Jesus into healing others. Which brings us squarely to face with our inability to forgive without Christ (Galatians 3:24). Forgiveness is supernatural; it takes a supernatural Source to tap into that power.

Fortunately, God has richly provided for us right at this point (Galatians 2:20). Even in our inner condemnation of the offender, we can come to Him on the cross, dying for our injustices, and His grace begins to flow! At the cross, we can experience our own forgiveness as well as tap into His divine ability to forgive others. As many times as it takes (Matthew 18:22).

THE CALL TO LOVE

I use the expression *Stay in your Lane*. Which means I only have control over me. Rarely if ever can I control another human being. But it is always my choice to love. And love conquers every obstacle.

Christian churches are riddled with violations regarding love. We have different visions, and suddenly there are hard feelings and accusations. People talk. People take sides. Friends walk away and maybe even become enemies. Sometimes we talk about these things at the dinner table, and give ourselves freedom to express our bitterness at home. This in turn infects our children. The cycle can stop with you.

We have to address the unspoken question: *Isn't there such a thing as righteous anger?* Yes there is. Jesus expressed His anger on a number of occasions, yet it was always when someone misrepresented His Father. Jesus felt God's emotion of anger, but He did not sin (Ephesians 4:26). On occasions like this we too may feel God's anger over a situation; our challenge in that moment is to first do business

148

with God before we do business *for* God. And here's the litmus test: if you can feel God's anger and still hear His voice and be under His control, then you're doing it right.

Most of the time, however, anger is our cue to throw ourselves upon divine mercy and receive His supernatural power to release and forgive. The closer we get to others in the church family, the more opportunity we will have to see something wrong in one another. Sooner or later you will be hurt, disappointed, or frustrated by someone in Christ's body. This is precisely when we need to be patient with each other, have faith for one another, and speak the kindest truth in the most genuine love. This is the Jesus Way.

DISCUSSION QUESTIONS

1. What is your instinctive response to authority figures in your life? Which do you easily trust...and which are harder to trust?

2. What is it like to voluntarily obey an authority that you don't entirely trust?

3. How good are you at forgiving people who have hurt you? Who do you still need to release from unforgiveness?

ELEVEN

Living on Purpose
Finding Your Place, Finding Your Way

When I was starting my first church in Fayetteville, I wanted to be a worship leader. I loved the presence of God. Hymns and worship songs never failed to stir my soul and draw my heart close to God. It felt like where I belonged. Naturally, I felt "called" to be a worship leader.

Acting on this instinct, I took guitar lessons and became fairly adept with chords, strumming, and even some picking. My sensitivity to the Holy Spirit and my heart to bring people into the presence of God inspired me and spurred me forward. When I took my guitar in front of the church to put this vision in motion, I felt like I came alive. Apparently, I was the only one.

The problem (or maybe I should say problems) was that I couldn't follow the musical flow and structure of the songs. I couldn't hear chord changes, and well, I didn't sing on key either. Other than those troubling details, I was a worship leader with a future.

Despite my shortcomings, our first church had no other worship leader in those early days. So I was it. And God used my willing heart for a season, even though I wasn't gifted, and eventually He sent people who were. I sometimes say that my lack of talent "provoked them to love and good works." Thank God for the Body of Christ and a multiplicity of giftings! God's intent is to connect us all together so that every need is covered.

Doing life with is all about that connection. Connection with God in redemption from the past and alignment with a purposeful future. And also connection with people so that we live in a vibrant spiritual community. Connection is the key to living on purpose. How does this work? Specifically, how do we find our fit in the Body of Christ? And how do we find our way when it comes to seeking guidance for the future?

151

God ingeniously pictures us as part of Christ's body—an eye, an ear, a hand, a finger, a foot, etc. (1 Corinthians 12:12-26). Part of growing up and gaining maturity is discovering how He designed us to function. We each have a place where we fit, a place that feels right and evokes satisfaction from being who we really are as we contribute to those God has placed around us.

My friend Mark was finishing his internship in India so I raised the question, *What's next?* "Well," he said, "I've learned that I'm not supposed to be the team leader, but I love being on the team." Good insight! That little piece of information is key to my friend finding out who he is, how God has wired him, and thus how he fits in the Body of Christ.

This is a journey that works best when we're *doing life with,* meaning it's your connection to God and then His people that shepherds you into this process of discovering who you are and how you fit.

It's a fascinating process to watch Jesus, as the Head, maneuver us into "our spot." As a church planter, I have had the joy of accompanying many people on this incredible journey, and I never tire of seeing firsthand the satisfaction people experience when the way they are wired connects with God's purpose.

The possibilities of personality and giftedness are wide open. Maybe you're an introvert and come alive in solitude...or the opposite: you feed on meeting new people. Some people are musical. Some thrive on creating order. Possibly details bore you to tears. Or you like to make things with your hands. Perhaps people just seem to gather around you. Or you love the adventure of initiating new paths; you get weary with maintaining old rhythms. Some people prefer to stay in the background. Maybe you love books, or you want to help someone else learn what you just learned.

God is the creative genius who uniquely designed you for your sweet spot—the sense that what you bring to the table somehow releases the gifts in others around you. It's His symbiotic miracle, putting people together who bring out the best in one another.

Clearly, the options are staggering, which is why it's important that we find where we belong. Every person has a place where gifts and talents shine. God made a lot of combinations, and only He has it figured out. So, how do we align our talents with opportunities in the community of faith?

THE MOTIVATION OF A SERVANT

God's starting place is always the same: assume the role of a servant. It's this desire to serve others that allows the Holy Spirit to use us in situation after situation, and along the way discover who we are and how we fit. "If anyone wants to be first, he shall be *servant of all*" (Mark 9:35, emphasis mine).

There are some wonderful things about servants. Servants are always welcome and aren't trying to prove themselves. Servants take pleasure in assisting others to fulfill their destiny without worrying so much about their own. Servants are humble, and God likes to hang out where there is humility. I tell those new to the faith, "don't go home as a prophet; go as a servant." No one was around to give me this needed wisdom when I first fell in love with Jesus.

So when you see a need, jump in and fill it. Even if it's not your true calling, you can bridge the gap until someone else picks up the ball. And as you search for your place in the community of faith, get feedback. It's amazing how God speaks to us through others.

In many churches today, the state-of-the-art has leapt forward in providing fairly structured and sophisticated ways to help people find their place. Small groups for newcomers. Coaches and mentors. Gift and aptitude inventories. Job fairs. Many times churches welcome people to experiment with different places of service until they find the one that fits best.

Whatever path your church provides, here are the keys to a successful fit:

- Come to give, not just receive.

- Be willing to try a task or position without getting possessive of it. If someone comes along who's better at it than you, give it away.

- Look for opportunities that touch on both your talent and your passion. That's a winning combination.

- Whatever your assignment in the community, build it around relationships and not just tasks.

- No matter how good you are or how long you've been doing it, never forget that it's all about serving.

RESPONDING TO THE LEADING OF GOD

When you join the community of faith, it begins as a place to receive and later to give. But the Body of Christ is more than that. The church is where we *do life with*. It's where we live and learn and grow and become. Part of that involves discerning God's will in your life. This involves two things: training your spiritual senses to hear God's voice for yourself and then learning to trust the larger community to confirm and fine-tune your hearing.

God is a Person, and He is far more relational than we are. Before Adam's disobedience, He walked with Adam and Eve in the cool of the evening, so it seems likely that they could see Him and hear Him in a tangible way. Sin ruptured this life-giving intimacy between Adam and God with the result that the two realms—this world and the realm in which God's authority has never been violated—were estranged from one another. Salvation is about bringing us back to God, restoring the relationship, and enabling us to function in His realm. This requires that we walk with Him once again and hear His voice.

When Jesus said, "My sheep hear My voice, and I know them, and they follow Me" (John 10:27), He was speaking of restoration to this long lost garden fellowship. It is a fellowship that our souls long for! We know our capacity for blundering along in life and making poor decisions; as Christ-followers we yearn to know that we're walking with Him where He is going.

We are, however, deeply accustomed to living in this world with our five physical senses, basing all decisions on the input they bring us. These senses clamor to dominate our attention. In contrast our spiritual senses are quiet, easily drowned out by the urgent, insistent, noisy world around us. Learning to listen to the still small voice of God requires both motivation and practice.

Just as God has given us the physical senses of sight, taste, touch, smell, and hearing, we have also been given spiritual senses. Just as we have natural sight, we have spiritual sight. His Spirit causes us to sense or perceive as if on an inner screen. You see a picture in your mind that you sense is more than imagination; it is a peering into the realm of the spirit. The true reality. Visions and dreams are particularly vivid pictures that can have their origin in the spiritual realm.

Spiritual hearing is the counterpoint to our natural hearing. Sometimes this impression is strong enough that we feel like we're actually hearing a divine voice, not often audible but distinctly within our perception. God does speak audibly in Scripture and sometimes even in our experience. But more often, we receive an inner thought, a sudden impression or unexpected insight that seems to have its origin outside ourselves. There is a quality about this type of hearing that is distinct, just as we recognize a friends' voice without seeing the person.

The psalmist sings, "O taste and see that the Lord is good; How blessed is the man who takes refuge in Him!" (Psalm 34:8). King David is experiencing the lavish abundance of God in such a way that he can only describe as a spiritual tasting. Even a spiritual feast! And Paul describes the God-inspired influence we have on the world as a "sweet aroma" (2 Corinthians 2:14-16).

The touch of God we might describe as an embrace of comfort or a nudge of guidance. Inner prompts may gently suggest a particular course of action. A divine nudge might be a sudden thought to call a person, go to a place, give someone money, do something for somebody, or even just notice a person.

Alternatively, God can give us a sense of caution, sort of a reverse nudge. A quiet, gentle sense of restraint that is meant to protect us from physical or spiritual harm. It can be a sense that maybe I shouldn't say that or make this decision or go to that event. It can be described as a lack of peace, understanding that God's peace is meant to rule our hearts and the lack of peace is often part of our internal guidance system (Colossians 3:15).

In addition there are times when the Spirit gives us an inner sense of just knowing something. A discernment that is not based upon natural facts but upon a spiritual discernment. For example you may have a sudden awareness that one person is going to marry another person or that someone is lying to you. You may suddenly know that a particular thing has happened or is going to happen. I often receive a clear sense of a man's calling when I first see him or shake his hand.

Unfortunately, all of these spiritual voices are easy to ignore when we are strong-willed and intense in our personalities or simply busy and preoccupied with the more natural voices around us. Learning to recognize and respond to divine prompts is part of growing up in Christ. We learn by trial and error, becoming stronger in discernment every time we choose correctly. We learn from our mistakes too.

UPGRADING OUR SPIRITUAL SENSES

How do we grow more intentionally in this ability to hear God's voice? The most basic, fundamental way of hearing God's voice is to read His word prayerfully, listening for Him to speak to us. "All Scripture is God-breathed and profitable for teaching, for reproof, for correction, for training in righteousness; so that the man of God may be adequate, equipped for every good work" says Paul in 2 Timothy 3:16-17.

The gold standard of how we evaluate God's voice is its agreement with His written word. We feed our spirit and prepare our minds to be able to hear God's voice by studying scripture, memorizing scripture, meditating upon scripture, and praying scripture. Keeping your daily appointment with God in order to spend time with Him is essential to developing your ability to hear His voice.

The Psalms speak of many ways in which we invest in our ability to hear His voice. For example, David challenges us to learn God's ways, observe His testimonies, take refuge in Him, and meditate upon

His laws. These are ways of paying attention to spiritual realities and cultivating active relationship with Father.

Paul speaks of sowing to the flesh or sowing to the spirit (Romans 8:5-7). This has to do with our willingness to forego our more immediate desires in exchange for tuning in to a higher wisdom. Regardless of how God's voice comes, our obedient response is the key to becoming more sensitized to hear more.

As children we have all heard our parents say, "You're not listening to me." In marriage we sometimes hear the same from our spouses. Learning to focus our attention upon the speaker has a way over time of increasing our ability to notice and respond, and every act of faith-obedience strengthens our relationship with God.

Receiving the Holy Spirit is another essential element for upgrading our spiritual senses, which we explored a few chapters ago. Praying in tongues on a daily basis is a way the apostle Paul suggests we strengthen our spirit (1 Corinthians 14:14-15), like exercising a spiritual muscle to make it stronger.

Put yourself in positions in which you need to hear the voice of the Spirit in order to advance the kingdom. Those who "seek first the kingdom" will be much more likely to hear the Savior's voice than those who are focused upon their own kingdom (Matthew 7:33). One of the most powerful is to obey Jesus' imperative to make disciples, and you will experience Him being with you in a unique way (Matthew 28:19-20).

Finally, keep a record of what He speaks to you. This demonstrates that you are serious about obeying what He says. One of the principles of the kingdom is the principle of stewardship. "For whoever has, to him more shall be given, and he will have an abundance" (Matthew 13:12). The Holy Spirit likes to entrust more to those who are motivated to reveal God's nature by serving others.

OBTAINING SPIRITUAL GUIDANCE

The quick way to reference God's means of guidance is to picture a ship entering a harbor by keeping four buoys lined up:

- Scripture.

- Witness of the Spirit.

- Circumstances.

- Authority.

For example, at some point it may be God's will for me to sell my house and move. Scripture has nothing to prevent me from doing this, so I check that off. Buoy number one. I will need a spiritual sense that it is God's will to sell my house, and I will need my wife to have the same sense. We need to be in agreement. Buoy number two.

Timing is always an issue in discerning God's will. If I put the house on the market, but can't find a buyer, then the time has not yet come. This circumstantial evidence is part of discerning God's direction and timing in my life. Buoy number three.

If I intend to move to another city, I will want to check with the spiritual authority over my life. In my case, there isn't one man, so I check with four spiritual men who know me well. If I am correctly sensing God's will, I expect all four men to agree with me. If some of them don't agree with my moving, then I will want to double down in seeking God to confirm the details. Buoy number four.

A number of years ago we followed this exact pattern in moving from Chapel Hill to Columbia. A strong prophetic word came in the middle of a gathering saying that I was supposed to go plant one more church. Although totally shocked, I had an immediate witness of the Spirit. In my gut, it felt like God.

Obviously this was a biblical proposal and one proven true in my life and ministry, so that was a green light. Then the circumstances lined up as I had taken a trip months earlier to Columbia to encourage a failed church plant, and I learned that several had been praying about my coming there. At the end of the day, I asked every senior leader and wife in our prophetic gathering to meet with us and to express his/her witness as to whether this was of God. They all said yes. So this was my authority. All four buoys lined up and led us to move within a matter of weeks.

We all make mistakes. We can move rashly by failing to either clarify a decision with God or confirm with trusted leaders and authorities. At other times we can become paralyzed by the fear of making a mistake and move too slowly. Fortunately He is a patient Teacher and is committed to bringing good results in the lives of those who are oriented toward His purposes.

THE AUTHORITY OF COMMUNITY

In the last chapter we explored God's idea of authority pretty extensively. And as we saw with the four buoys, authority is one of the key touchpoints to guide solid decision-making on the larger questions of life. Now let's expand on that idea just a bit.

Scripture says that "without consultation, plans are frustrated, But with many counselors they succeed" (Proverbs 15:22). Remember, none of us is meant to go it alone. We all need each other in many vital ways. So when it comes to discerning God's guidance in our lives, it should be no surprise that His wisdom emerges best from our togetherness.

My friend Michael Cotten says: *If you and your wife are one flesh, you can expect half of everything God wants to say to you to come through her.* So if you're married, your community discernment begins with your spouse.

Where does it go next?

Well, who is most vested in your life? Who carries a spiritual gift of wisdom? Whose spiritual path do you admire most? Who have you come to trust with the in's and out's of your past experiences? These questions will help you know who to invite into your discernment process.

It's also important to not "shop for counsel," going only to the people most likely to agree with us. By screening input for our preferred content, we defeat the process and avoid the breadth of wisdom God may wish to bring us through trusted counselors.

In addition, God has established some with spiritual authority in each of our lives by virtue of the person's position. These people include your pastor or elder or small group leader. Such leaders are held to a high level of spiritual accountability—by God (James 3:1) and hopefully also by the community. Hebrews 13:17 reminds us to "obey your leaders and submit to them, for they keep watch over your souls as those who will give an account." The counsel of these people should carry special weight.

If we are not pursuing God's will for our lives in very purposeful ways, we need to ask ourselves, *Am I doing God's will or my own will?* Too often what seems good in my own mind is merely a reflection of what feels comfortable in the moment...or appears to be in my own best interests...or is simply expedient. God's heart for our good is much grander than such small measures.

This is a new way of thinking for many of us, so I invite you to consider who belongs in your discernment community and how we can help one another find our way together toward the full purposes of God.

DISCUSSION QUESTIONS

1. How well have you found your "fit" in the Body of Christ? How easy is it for you to take the role of a servant to others?

2. In what ways are you hearing God's voice? Which spiritual senses are most active in your life now?

3. How have you experienced God's protection for your life through the wise counsel of spiritual authorities?

4. Read Hebrews 13:17 with fresh ears, listening for God's application to your own life. "Obey your leaders and submit to them, for they keep watch over your souls as those who will give an account. Let them do this with joy and not with grief, for this would be unprofitable for you." How is this dynamic working in your life?

TWELVE

Work as Worship
Reclaiming our Divine Partnership

I was in for a rude awakening. It was June of 1968, and Jesus had become by far the most important thing in my life. My job flying for the Air Force no longer seemed to matter, so I didn't see this coming. The Spirit interrupted me one day with this attention-getter: "If you don't buckle down and do a better job with your current responsibilities, I'm not going to let you out of the Air Force." Knowing I was called to preach, I was caught off guard by this correction. But I knew this voice and obeyed promptly.

What does work have to do with the kingdom of God? I never heard this question addressed by the church in my early years of following Jesus. We sang, "This world is not my home, we're just passing through." We heard a lot about not being "of the world," and the implication was that while church work was eternal, the marketplace was mere necessity. Just a means of paying the bills.

The message that *work is worship*—or perhaps I should say that work is *intended to be* worship—is largely neglected in the church. Maybe we missed the memo.

In our culture, change is endemic. Paradigm shifts are daily news. iPhones and iPads have merely prepared us for the buzz on smart watches and computer glasses. By the time you read this, those will be old news and we'll be on to the next new thing. Meanwhile, the church is beginning to shake off its dusty moorings and awaken to a lifestyle of serious, accelerated change. A lot of the catching up has to do with technology, but it's far more than that. It's a new way of thinking and anticipating. Innovation is the new normal. The multi-site church is the most recent adaptation to our changing culture, which will soon give place to yet more transformations.

But in the midst of all this change trauma the church has a resource that our culture cannot decipher: the Body of Christ. The

Body is beginning to wake up to its powerful calling: *its divine partnership on planet earth that includes God's purpose for work.* Society understands work as necessity, identity, and survival, but only God's friends realize that we are privileged to find meaning and destiny as His co-workers. Our God works, and He created us to accompany Him as the stewards of creation in our work.

Listen to God's first words to Adam and Even in the Garden: "Be fruitful and multiply, and fill the earth, and subdue it; and rule over the fish of the sea and over the birds of the sky, and over every living thing that moves on the earth" (Genesis 1:28). Often called the "Cultural Mandate," this was the charge for humanity as they entered the world—and it remains a call to co-create with God in the world.

It's not just the animals we are called to rule; commerce, society, government, the arts, and now global relations—all of these fall into the human-divine partnership God intended from day one.

Christian innovators have been pushing the envelope with B4T (Business for Transformation), but while this quiet movement is transforming international ministry, the church world seems largely unaware. It will not be long before the Spirit of God breaks into our ranks with an unexpected revolution: ordinary Christians creating businesses for the glory of God and the advancement of the kingdom! The priesthood of the believers is about to invade the marketplace.

It's not surprising that the B4T innovators have come from the fringes of the mission field, nor that they have experienced the ineffectiveness of "the church in the bubble." The newly energized American church today breathes a similar pragmatic air. It works. Business is God's idea. The church, like Jesus, is soon to be about our Father's business.

A KINGDOM CALLING

Nan and I were recently introducing ourselves to three other couples, and the question went around the table, "Are you retired?" They all said yes but us. Of course they asked what I did, and when I told them, the telling comment came, "Oh, you have a calling. That's different."

Jesus' invitation is to all, "Come follow Me, and I will make you fishers of men." This is both a calling and a destiny, regardless of our differing assignments. In a biblical sense there is no vocation without calling, no career track without a calling. Whether you are a plumber, a physician, or a pastor, you are invited into your profession at God's initiative. All work is a "following after Jesus," and all is ripe with Kingdom potential.

Imagine a local church filled with teachers and small business owners and electricians and financial advisors and salespeople and computer programmers—all carrying a sense of divine purpose and partnership into their workplaces. They get up in the morning excited about meaningful conversations with clients, water cooler "pastoring" of their co-workers, leading a lunchtime Bible study, and discipling a new Christian who works a couple cubicles down.

These men and women have no seminary degrees; they just burn with God's love for people and are bold to express that care in ways that fit their personalities and giftings. Now imagine all the local churches in your city equipping its people for this kind of kingdom invasion of the marketplace.

This is precisely what Jesus had in mind when He spoke those famous words, "Go therefore and make disciples of all the nations, baptizing them in the name of the Father and the Son and the Holy Spirit, teaching them to observe all that I commanded you" (Matthew 28:19-20). That command was never intended to merely be the domain of professional ministers—that would be an impossibility! But when all God's children take the Father's heart with them into the local post office, bank, and office complex, that's when a social revolution begins. This is God's dream for changing the world, and each of us is a key player.

So what is your calling? How has God spent your entire lifetime preparing you to serve Him? What background, what education, what passion does He intend to harness in the marketplace that will function as a conduit for expressing His love and care to others? Chances are good that the men and women God puts on your radar in your workplace will not be in church to hear this Sunday's sermon. Instead, they will watch the sermon of your life and hear Father's kindness expressed through your mouth.

CALLING ALIGNMENT

Maybe you're thinking that there is nothing in your workplace that excites you. You care about the people there, but the work itself is meaningless. This is probably an indication that you haven't yet found your calling. Despite the relational opportunities available in any work environment, there is always the work itself. That is not insignificant.

We need to grasp that a calling begins with the work. Maybe you're an orthodontist, and you spend your days putting wires in the mouths of teenagers. Or you're a plumber, and your work finds you on your back under clogged sinks and in dirty crawl spaces under houses. What is the kingdom significance of straight teeth and toilets that flush? A lot. Producing goods and services that people are willing to pay for means that you are generating value in the human family. You play a vital role in the community's health and happiness. This is part of the Cultural Mandate and God's personal assignment to you.

Paul spoke directly to this truth: "Whatever you do, work at it with all your heart, as working for the Lord, not for human masters, since you know that you will receive an inheritance from the Lord as a reward. It is the Lord Christ you are serving" (Colossians 3:23-24).

Work is meant to align with your unique abilities and interests. Some people are genuinely fascinated with fixing computers; they love the way computers work and are energized by the challenge of a broken laptop. Others would rather be beaten with a stick than try to load a printer driver. Some folks love to sell things, anything, while others would consider that an early visit to purgatory.

My granddaughter Abbie loved nothing more in grade school than the annual fundraiser when she would get to walk door-to-door through her neighborhood and sell wrapping paper or cookie dough. She thrived on the task of visiting as many houses as possible, the challenge of making that personal connection in seconds, the thrill of closing the deal, and the competition for the price that went to the top seller in her grade. It fit her wiring and reflects something of her life calling—something yet to be fully revealed.

Thousands of people are capable in their work yet live for the weekend. The tasks they face each day feel meaningless because they see no vital connection with God's calling. No sense of vocation. They dread Monday mornings, talk about getting past "hump day"—the midpoint of the week—and then try to accelerate the clock through Thursday and Friday with dreams of the fun they will finally have come Saturday. This is not only a tragic way to live but contrary to our divine design. You can't live that way for long without doing damage to your soul.

TGIF (Thank God It's Friday) is meant to be more about satisfaction than relief—the conclusion of work well done, the contentment of having shown up as God's representative in our work world and faithfully carried that torch another week.

PURSUE THE JOY

Even when your vocation is rightly aligned—when you're doing the kind of work you are called to— you still may not love everything equally. No matter how perfect the job, there will always be some tasks that aren't fun; they simply have to be done. And there will be tasks you do like that, due to various circumstances, get obstructed or sabotaged or wearisome or frustrating. This is life on planet earth, and there is something inside us that knows we are made for heaven.

But when our vocations are aligned with our divine design, then our most enduring experience of that work is joy. We're doing what we're made for, and that speaks to something deep in the soul—something God put there. Remember Eric Liddell, the Scottish Olympian in the movie *Chariots of Fire*? When challenged by his well-meaning sister about neglecting his missionary work, he replied, "I believe God made me for a purpose, but he also made me fast. And when I run I feel His pleasure."

Any father who watches his child tap into a vein of talent and excel, whether it's in athletics or academics or art, feels a surge of pleasure in the child's joy. That is simply a reflection of the Father's heart toward you. If you rarely feel God's pleasure in your joyful work, it's time for a change.

If you hate your work, then part of partnering with God in the world involves finding new work. And in some locations and economies that's tough. But since vocation is supernatural, you can expect God to show up and lead you to a place that fits. There may be a need for a season of prayer and seeking, understanding that sometimes that season may be longer than we like. Yet God uses such seasons to build into us the patience and perseverance He knows we need. He is always equipping us, sometimes in ways we would not choose. But whatever the situation, don't let go of the pursuit! Remember, God's will is for you to have alignment between your calling and your work.

A KINGDOM PERSPECTIVE ON RETIREMENT

Just as some unhappy workers live for the weekend, others live for retirement. There can easily be the feeling that "I've put in my time slaving for others; now it's time for me!" But again, this would be to miss God's perspective on both work and retirement.

What we call retirement is, from a kingdom viewpoint, simply a transition to God's next assignment. If you have been engaged in a career that was a God-inspired vocation, then coming to the conclusion of that stage is reason for celebration—not because you finally get to quit, but because of all that God did in and through you during those years. You were productive. You were joyful. You provided for your family and lives were changed. Celebration indeed!

Retirement may legitimately bring with it a slower pace and more time for grandchildren, travel, and other enjoyable pursuits, but there is one thing that retirement cannot be: as long as we belong to God, this new season cannot be a time to simply indulge ourselves. Rather, retirement can usher us into our most productive kingdom season ever.

The combination of financial freedom, physical health, and time autonomy is an amazing blend of availability to serve in ways that may not have been possible during your career. While the job is over, your calling remains. During your latter years you may find various new joyful ways to live it out.

The greatest threat to a joyful, productive retirement is a shortfall on either the financial side or the health side, and both of these hinge largely upon wise preparations during the career season. So for those still in that time of life, it's good to steward those resources in a God-honoring way…which is the subject of our next chapter.

DISCUSSION QUESTIONS

1. What is your sense of God's purpose in your current work or school or life situation?

2. How would you describe your calling?

3. What percentage of your typical day taps your passion and brings you joy? Seeing that number, how do you feel about that?

THIRTEEN

Kingdom Resources
Becoming Good Stewards

Tithing, to use an old expression, was "in my mother's milk." Growing up in a traditional, small, southern town it was just part of the fabric of life to attend church on Sunday and to pay your tithe. For the Daley family, giving 10% of our income to the church was part of our family DNA, even before our family became believers. I never questioned it; it was a given.

I inherited stories of a grandfather I never knew who strongly held to several beliefs regarding the tithe: 1) that to withhold the first 10% from God was robbing Him, 2) that tithing was an honorable way to test God to pour out His blessings, and 3) that God would rebuke the devourer of one's goods on behalf of the one who obeyed God through the tithe (Malachi 3:8-12).

The fact that Mr. Thorpe rose from near poverty to some wealth validated his belief in God's promises for our family. The story holds that he requested in his will for all his children to tithe on anything they received from him. As far as I know, they did!

The bad news is that we knew far more about tithing than about knowing God. My father married into this family tradition, and he tithed as "the right thing to do." I remember asking him when I was sixteen, "Dad, why are we here? What's our purpose?" His frank answer was, "Son, I've wondered that for a long time; I thought I would know the answer by the time I was 40, but I don't."

Dad experienced the power of tithing years before he would become a follower of Christ. He started Builder's Hardware at Five Points in Rocky Mount, North Carolina, before World War II broke out. The problem with owning a hardware store during the war was that all manufacturing went into the war effort; there wasn't much to sell.

In 1943 Dad volunteered for the Army and was providentially stationed right where most of his hardware was being manufactured, although precious little of it was available. He then became good friends with the regional salesman and stayed in his house on weekends. Because of this friendship, Dad's business received far more hardware than anybody else. So even while he was away, his little store made more money than ever before. It was a beginning.

I never knew my grandfather, but I thank God for his legacy of prayer, faith, and obedience. I suspect that in the mystery of how God works, he played some part in God putting a hunger in our hearts for knowing Him, for being close to Him. As soon as we were introduced to Christ as our personal Savior, we found that the path to honoring God with the first 10% of our income was already carved out for us. He left us an inheritance that would ripple through generations.

My search for God during my first duty station turned out to be an extension of my 16-year-old question, "Why am I here? What's my purpose?" Of course my initial encounter with God as my own Father far exceeded all my expectations. I was stunned by the experience of being known, loved, and secured by my heavenly Father. Purpose flowed so naturally that I hardly noticed it. He was everything; and I wanted to surrender everything I had to Him for Him.

Stewardship is the natural response to knowing Father. We just want to join Him in what He's doing with everything at our disposal. The word "steward" is closely connected to this sense of life purpose. It is a powerful concept that speaks directly to our identity and calling as the Father's children in this world. "One who manages the property, finances, and affairs for the owner": that's the definition and that's our assignment from God.

In Genesis 1:26 Adam and Eve were given their very first stewardship—the very image of God by which they would represent God in this new world. To be a steward of God Himself is the highest honor! And as stewards, they were given a tangible mandate: be fruitful, multiply, fill, subdue, and rule. This mandate and this stewardship continue on to us today (Genesis 1:28).

Except that we have a problem. There's nothing worse than when a steward begins to think he or she is the owner. Paul asked the

Corinthians pointedly, "What do you have that you did not receive?" (1 Corinthians 4:7). The answer, of course, is nothing. You and I are placed in this world to manage God's property, His finances, and His affairs until He returns. Miss this, and…well, we miss the point of life!

Jesus told a very intense, no-holds-barred story about what it means to be God's steward. The RSV translates it properly, "There was a rich man who had a steward and charges were brought to him that this man was wasting his goods" (Luke 16:1-2). The "rich man" represents God, and the steward represents us, His people.

The Owner says to the steward, "Render the accounting of your stewardship." Jesus then shocked His listeners by describing this unfaithful steward as a dishonest man who receives a commendation! How could this be? Because this steward was thinking of the future and how he would fare. And that was Jesus' point: effective stewardship with what we have been entrusted requires us to look ahead, think ahead, and plan ahead.

As a master storyteller, Jesus intentionally seized everyone's attention with this story, making the "bad guy" the "good guy." And His challenge to us is equally provocative and equally clear: use your resources to benefit people, investing for long-term returns.

It was a frequent topic for Jesus: who and what will you serve? And He simplifies our choices; God or money—which one will it be? (Luke 16:13). In the Sermon on the Mount, Jesus connects this issue of Lordship with our deepest priorities as well as the whole issue of worry about provision (Matthew 6:19-34). The bottom line? "Your heavenly Father knows that you need all these things. But seek first His kingdom and His righteousness, and all these things will be added to you" (Matthew 6:32-33).

It's an incredible joy to live life as God's steward, God's partner, and to experience His provision for all the practical needs we face each day.

How do we know if we are seeking His kingdom first? While many things can contribute to the answer, perhaps nothing cuts to the chase as fast as our calendars and our wallets. When you look at how people spend their time and money, it's pretty evident where their priorities lie and whether those priorities are aligned with God's kingdom or their own.

STEWARDING OUR MONEY

Let's start with money. Jesus was not bashful about challenging His listeners on this topic. In the Old Testament God's requirements about money were embedded in the sacrificial system of paying a tithe—ten percent—of currency, livestock, and produce from the field. Abraham honored Melchizedek, a shadowy type of Christ in Genesis 14:17-20, with ten percent of his plunder from a conquered king. Later God codified the tithe in the Mosaic Law, a precise accounting of the principle of stewardship that stood for the next several thousand years.

When Jesus entered the scene, he did not emphasize the practice in his teaching, leading many Christians today to believe that the tithe is no longer commanded or expected by God. I disagree. The reason Jesus did not emphasize the tithe is that the Jews of His day were not questioning it; in other words, there was no argument and no need to address it. They all believed and practiced the tithe.

Jesus did, however, need to question the motives of the Pharisees who tithed scrupulously but failed to represent God's heart in pursuing justice. "But woe to you Pharisees! For you pay tithes of mint and rue and every kind of garden herb, and yet disregard justice and the love of God; but these things you should have done without neglecting the others" (Luke 11:42).

In this Jesus gets to the heart of how we represent God and the priorities of the kingdom (the stewardship of the image of God) while validating the matter of paying the tithe (the stewardship of our finances)! The tithe was commanded in the Old Testament and never rescinded. Which leads us to understand that the matter of stewardship is more than the issue of tithing, but it's not less.

All our resources belong to God. All income comes from Him, regardless of our role in it. Paying Him the first ten percent of all our income is a loud statement that He alone is our Source, that He is the Owner, we the stewards.

When we read Malachi 3:7f today, we rarely have the background information to process it as the first hearers would have. This is a strong rebuke and appeal from the Father-heart of God to His children.

> "From the days of your fathers you have turned aside from My statutes and have not kept them. Return to Me, and I will return to you," says the Lord of hosts.
>
> "But you say, 'How shall we return?'" [Note God's answer.]
>
> "Will a man rob God?" [Pretty strong.] "Yet you are robbing Me! But you say, 'How have we robbed You?' In tithes and offerings."
>
> "You are cursed with a curse, for you are robbing Me.... Bring the whole tithe into the storehouse, so that there may be food in My house, and test Me now in this," says the Lord of hosts, "if I will not open for you the windows of heaven and pour out for you a blessing until it overflows."
>
> "Then I will rebuke the devourer for you, so that it may not destroy the fruits of the ground; nor will your vine in the field cast its grapes," says the Lord of hosts.
>
> "All the nations will call you blessed, for you shall be a delightful land," says the Lord of hosts.

Normally the idea of testing God is an act of accusing and judging God. Satan likes this. God doesn't. But here God Himself unexpectedly invites us to test Him and see if He will not keep His word. No wonder Satan hates for us to honor God with our first ten percent as well as additional offerings. We are His servants and His stewards, and the tithe represents this beautifully! Who would want to forego these wonderful promises?

STEWARDING OUR TIME

While the stewardship of money is represented by a very exact percentage, our management of time is more complicated...yet no less vital to our stewardship. Every minute and every hour we have been given in life belongs to God. We recognize and honor this truth when we allow Him to govern our use of it, just as with our money.

The Sabbath was the Old Testament commandment that highlighted this priority, another practice that Jesus upheld. The Sabbath was also spiritualized in Hebrews 4 as a picture of living in His rest by receiving the accomplishments of Christ as our justification before God rather than our human efforts. Yet the stewardship remains.

As with our money, we set aside certain portions of our time as a "sacrifice" of worship while seeking to honor the Owner of our time in how we utilize the rest of it. Apart from worship and serving in the church and the community, we are tasked with investing the remainder of our time in things that yield a high "rate of return" in eternal measures.

Jesus' parable of the Talents demonstrates even more of His view on stewardship. In this case a wealthy Owner distributes money to be managed by three stewards—and it's not an equal distribution! One receives five talents, another two, and another merely one. The five-talent and two-talent stewards invest their resources and double their value before the Owner returns, yet the one-talent steward hides his resource in fear of failure—not to mention his harsh view of the Owner.

Jesus comes down hard on this epic failure of stewardship, reinforcing the centrality and importance of our role as managers of kingdom resources. When it comes to money, we all get different portions—and the portion is not as important as the stewardship. Time, however, is another thing. When it comes to the clock, the playing field is level. Every human gets the same number of hours in a day, though not the same number of years in a life. The point? Use them as the Master would. To love God and love our neighbor.

OTHER KINGDOM RESOURCES

The word "talent" in the New Testament was a measure of money, a currency note, but our modern use of the word fits the profile of stewardship well. We don't all have the same aptitudes, passions, natural abilities, or spiritual gifts; yet our collection of these forms the "talent" entrusted to us and belongs to the kingdom of God.

Our talents and abilities are meant to be invested in alignment with the values of heaven—not merely for our own enjoyment and advancement but for the greater good of God's children. Our talents will probably play a part in how we make a living in this world; that's a good thing. But they also belong to the Master and have been uniquely crafted and given to us to implement at His bidding.

Our bodies, Paul says, are the "temple of the Holy Spirit" (1 Corinthians 6:19). Our physical body is another kingdom resource entrusted to our stewardship. To dishonor or abuse this gift is tantamount to "burying our talent," or worse, squandering it outright. Like time and money, our bodies are temporal—they will come and go. Nonetheless, while they are in our hands and under our care, they are a powerful tool for fulfilling the purposes of God in the world. Our bodies are tasked with carrying our souls and our divine calling for 80 or 90 years or better. What we don't want is for our body to run short of our calling!

This leads to a very practical set of considerations regarding how we eat, how we exercise, how much we weigh, and our use of substances that might compromise our quantity and quality of life. We are each a steward of our God-given temple, and whatever choices we make concerning the care of these bodies, we will live (hopefully) with the results.

Money, time, talents, health, energy, affection, intelligence, experience—all are gifts of God. All are resources to be used for God's purposes. All have been given to us to steward. As sons, daughters, and servants, let us manage them well!

DISCUSSION QUESTIONS

1. What are your impressions around this idea of being a steward of God's resources?

2. How would God's priorities be reflected in your checkbook?

3. How would God's priorities be reflected in your calendar?

4. How would God's priorities be reflected in your physical health?

FOURTEEN

So Now What?
The Logistics of Disciple-Making

If we could put a stethoscope on the souls of people, we would hear the near-silent swish of the human heart saying, "Who will teach me to be a man? Who will show me what it means to be a woman? Who will father me, coach me, show me how to make life work?"

Just as we don't hear the swish of our physical heart until someone comes along with a stethoscope, we aren't even aware of this inner yearning until God sends someone to us who is a little older and trained to listen. You won't spot him with a stethoscope around his neck, but you will see him paying attention to someone younger, seeing the potential, and offering to be a coach through the simple act of listening.

I'm not at all sure I knew what I was doing when I first laid eyes on a sandy-red-haired, 18-year-old, 82nd Airborne soldier named Jim Laffoon, but there was something in him, a calling, a potential. Although I couldn't have defined it, I saw it and felt it and wanted to see it come forth.

Now 60 years of age Jim said to me recently, "You were the first person after my parents who believed in me. You taught me about God, about marriage, and about life." I think my first question to him as a young man was a blunt, "What has God called you to do?" If you know Jim, you know how powerfully God has used him as a prophet and teacher, although at the time we met he had other ideas. I think the Father chuckles with us as He reshapes us and surprises us with the joy of working alongside Him.

Jesus watched His heavenly Father in order to recognize the men He was to disciple, but once He invited them, they had to choose. To follow or not. We may have to express our interest in a man several times before we are certain this is God's connection for us (since we may not be as tuned in as Jesus was), but it is still necessary that the relationship involve mutual commitment. Like the original twelve, Jim Laffoon was quick to respond; he wanted to be with me.

Years ago I was preparing for a triathlon and needed to improve my skill as a swimmer. When I discovered a woman on staff at the local YMCA who had been a competitive swimmer in college, I asked her, "Would you be willing to teach me?" I was thrilled when she eagerly took me on as a pupil. How amazing that she would invest in me when it was neither her job nor of any financial benefit to her. Needless to say, she did not have to track me down or motivate me. She was serving me, and I was the grateful recipient.

Every coach also knows the opposite: a young man shows up brimming with potential but somehow lacks the fire in his belly to commit, to be on time, to do the work. Coaches love to inspire young people to become their best, but there is one quality they cannot supply: faithfulness. Paul told Timothy to entrust the message and mission to "faithful men" (2 Timothy 2:2). When a man is not faithful, I don't stop caring about him, but I can't equip him to fulfill his destiny. Sometimes we have to wait for God to do something in people's hearts before they're ready to be trained. And the best thing we can do in that in-between time is to back off and give them time and space.

START WITH STORY

Every person has a story, and I want to know it. The fact that I am interested, that I want to know the details, the background, that I ask the questions and listen intently is very likely to be a first-time experience for the guys I mentor. And of course my interest must be deeply genuine, not just a technique. You can't fake disciple-making.

In this relationship I am the Question-Man. *Tell me about your parents. Where did you grow up? Which child were you? What was it like growing up in your family? Why did you feel that way? What things have impacted you the most?* All the while I am listening carefully for the Holy Spirit's sense of where to go with the next question as well as how to interpret what I'm hearing. This is the approach I recommend to other disciplers.

We all are a huge container of experiences, disappointments, victories, failures, surprises, scars, dreams, and fears. It tends to be a chaotic jumble because most people haven't been able to process their lives. Hopefully you will be the father figure (or mother figure) who will help a younger person integrate those things that have shaped her life. She needs you as the outsider to help her connect the dots and give insights that prove to be both healing and faith-building. In many cases, you may find yourself doing for another person what you wish someone had done for you. This is a description of mentoring.

EXPLORE THE GOD-CONNECTION

The primary goal is for this person to know God.

I often ask, "When do you pray? How do you pray? What are you experiencing?" I need to find out what his relationship with Father is really like. God Himself is the ultimate source, and my constant emphasis will be upon helping a man meet with and experience God as his Father. This is the relationship Jesus modeled for us, and it was His mission to bring us into the same quality of sonship He enjoyed.

I then invite a disciple into my own devotional life with Father, and I encourage you to do the same. He needs to see that it is the life of God in me that makes me tick. I don't have devotions out of an "ought" but because I can't live without His impartation of life into me every morning. I follow David who says, "In the morning, O Lord, You will hear my voice; In the morning I will order my prayer to You and eagerly watch" (Psalm 5:3).

I show him how I journal, how I "pray read" the Psalms, how I interact with Scripture using my marking pen, and how I meditate upon a passage or wait upon God. I am basically taking this man with me into life.

We never outgrow our need for intimacy with Christ. The mark of maturity is increasing humility, increasing dependency upon Christ in me. I smile when I think of my trainer from Gold's Gym, Troy Hines. What a joy it is to see the fruit that God is bearing through his life, knowing I had a part in discipling him during his first few years of following Christ. Today we are great friends, and whenever we meet I ask, "What's God saying to you?" And he has an immediate answer. He got it; you can see Christ in him as a result. This is what God wants in every disciple.

BALANCE CONTENT AND QUESTIONS

Part of the discipleship process is laying foundations by introducing truths that this person has never known or understood before. Another part of the process is in responding to the spontaneous questions of the disciple's heart, inspired by where she is in her unique journey. So your job is to manage both of these dynamics: to take the initiative to teach and to respond to the organic opportunities that emerge.

Content-wise, this book will be your guide. The last twelve chapters will be your starting point for laying a solid spiritual foundation for both principles and practice in this person's life. Certain topics may arise that will lead you to other resources that go deeper in one facet or another; then you can return here.

So when do you ask questions and when do you give answers?

Show and tell is the primary teaching tool for children. We show them how to do tasks—whether it's tying a shoe, brushing their teeth, or praying. We also tell them how to behave and what to avoid, but as a child matures, the most powerful learning tool becomes self-discovery.

I'm always watching for "the teachable moment"—that situation, that moment when someone wants to know something, wants to change something in his or her life. When a person feels needy or vulnerable, that's when it's time to hand over the right tool. An insight. A word of wisdom. A suggestion. A heart-opening question. Maybe a different interpretation of what he is experiencing; this is called *reframing*, and it can be a game-changer to offer a fresh perspective in place of an old one.

Listening, asking questions, offering wisdom: this is an art form developed from listening to your disciple and to the Holy Spirit at the same time. Sometimes the best thing you can do for your disciple is ask, "What is the next step of growth God wants you to take in your ministry?" That may open up an entirely new arena of conversation, reading, prayer, and movement.

INSTIGATE OUTSIDE LEARNING

Every time you meet with your disciple, you want to give a specific assignment that forms the starting point for your next meeting. The right assignments lead to rich discoveries. Homework gives a disciple something extremely tangible to do, something intimately connected to the growth points in his life currently. Keep it simple and straightforward. Something specific and due by a certain date. This type of action and follow-up is vital to his growth.

To a young man newly married: "The next time we meet, I want you to tell me how you and your wife planned to go to bed earlier so you can have time together with God before you launch into your day."

To a mission worker who needs to improve her marriage: "This week I want you to journal my three questions about the emotions you've experienced in the last 24 hours. I want you two to share and discuss your answers with one another."

To a teenager: "This week I want you to go to your parents and ask forgiveness for the specific ways you have dishonored them. We'll talk about it when that's accomplished."

To an office worker who feels fearful sharing his faith: "Learn the names of the children of two of your co-workers and ask how you can pray for them."

To a husband who wants a stronger marriage: "This week I want you to make a list of the five Love Languages and describe how you are expressing all five love languages to your wife."

To a construction worker who feels she's been a poor witness by her attitude toward the job: "Tell your boss and two closest co-workers that as a disciple of Jesus, you do not think your work has been a good example of your faith. Ask their forgiveness and then ask how they think you can improve your job performance."

To someone struggling with the grace of God: "I would like for you to journal through your time with the Father for the next seven days, focusing on His enjoyment of you.

I will commonly assign a disciple to read two chapters in a book so we can discuss his insights the following week and find out how this is working in his life. If the disciple is overweight or undisciplined in some area of life, I talk about diet, exercise, sleep, use of time, and margins. Then together we will set specific goals for change.

When you discuss the disciple's homework, you're looking for several things: the "aha" moments, the points of confusion, and the opportunities for more dialogue. Plus you're evaluating the assignment itself: was it too little, too complicated, not clear enough, or just right? Adapt what you are learning about your disciple so as to make the next assignment a better fit.

Scripture memory, meditation, spouse assignments, journaling, job performance, seeking reconciliation, logging exercise, financial budgeting, updates on children and parenting changes—all these can be strategic assignments that move your disciple forward.

FIND A GOOD RELATIONAL RHYTHM

How often should you meet? It depends on what the disciple is experiencing in life. If she is a brand new follower of Christ, it may be wise to check in every day for a short conversation. In addition invest at least one solid hour each week.

Sometimes the assignments you give lend themselves to meeting every other week. Scheduling depends upon the maturity and availability of the person. Personally, I meet with some every week, some every other week, and others once a month.

Whatever fits your disciple, it's good to establish a routine, a regularity that promotes the transformational process. So, after experimenting for a bit, settle into a groove and stick with it.

CHOOSE A LOCATION

Coffee shops are usually a favorite place to connect. Other times you can meet over lunch or at home. Sometimes you have to talk by cell or Skype, but in person is better. Observing your disciple in an everyday work environment can also be helpful to see dynamics firsthand, so many times I have taken a sack lunch to eat with a man at his job site. Sometimes we get time together by going for walks or hikes.

Basically you're looking for a place that is convenient to access and where it's easy to talk. Something to eat or drink helps build a sense of community. Doing a simple activity may also provide something to occupy the body while you connect at a heart level.

It's helpful to do something fun with those you mentor; not everything has to be serious. Learning to enjoy people in different settings is powerful and really is a way of *doing life with* them. It's part of being real, part of being human, of welcoming another person into your own life and taking your place in theirs. Each different environment tends to open up new dimensions of the person and the relationship.

BUILD IN ACCOUNTABILITY

It's not unusual for someone to fail to complete an assignment. The question in that moment is, *How will you hold this person accountable in a way that is affirming and inspires faith?* When we ask ourselves the question this way the Holy Spirit will give us wisdom that accomplishes all three things: holding him accountable, affirming him, and inspiring faith that he can do this.

Sometimes, however, this isn't enough. Occasionally and with certain folks the "old coaching" method is required. Sometimes you have to challenge people strongly and directly. This is not the starting point in a discipling relationship, but sometimes it takes a wake-up call or a come-to-Jesus-moment to get someone's attention and challenge old patterns. Sometimes this is what love looks like (Matthew 23:17).

When someone does not do the assignment, it may be helpful to step back and ask yourself the question *Why?* Perhaps you need to pay attention to an underlying issue in her life. Her failure may be the Holy Spirit's way of highlighting an old wound, a particular sin pattern, or something that needs to come into the light. This can become a special opportunity to provide the mentoring she needed but has not received.

PLAN TO MULTIPLY

Understand that *making disciples is about the second grader helping the first grader learn his lessons.* The sooner your disciple begins to help another man grow, the faster he will himself grow. Jesus' command to "go therefore and make disciples" cannot start too soon in a convert's life.

Envision him with this lifetime calling—to help others grow spiritually. Help him look at those God has placed around his life and notice someone he might be able to mentor. Once your disciple secures his own disciple, you will watch the whole dynamic take on a rich new depth and beauty!

BE REAL

One of the pitfalls that people sometimes fall into once they begin to disciple another is the mistaken notion that now they have to be the one with all the answers. Or the one who has already integrated everything you've just taught. Of course once we name this tendency, we can see how foolish it is. No matter how young or seasoned we are as Christ-followers, we are still learning too!

It is intrinsically trust-building to appropriately share your own struggles and stretching points with the person you're discipling. This invites him or her into your learning as well as models the reality of discipleship as a life-long process. Transparency is part and parcel of humility; you will find that it strengthens the relationship rather than undermines it. Also expect to learn from your disciple, just as we often learn from our children.

Finally, it's okay not to know all the answers. Sometimes a question might be wisely answered with, "You know, I really don't know the answer to that. Let me do a little research and see what I can find. Let's talk about that next week." At other times there just isn't an easy answer to be had! *Why did my infant nephew die after receiving prayer? Why did I get passed over for that last promotion?* There are some biblical truths that we can draw upon in painful situations, but it is a priceless act of worship to bow before the mystery and majesty of God in our un-knowing. The sovereignty of God is meant to bring us to trust, not always to understanding.

Ready to get started?

DISCUSSION QUESTIONS

1. Who has been a spiritual father or mother in your life? How has that investment shaped who you are today?

2. What excites you most about being a spiritual father / mother to others now? Where do you feel resistance or anxiety?

3. By personality are you more of a "teller" or "asker" in relationships? Which would you like to strengthen in your disciple-making?

Doing Life With

FIFTEEN

Doing Life With
Let's Get Started

My message from page one in this book is that we, like the children of the President, have been given the run of the place. The "West Wing" of the kingdom of God is our playground, and—unlike the President's children—we have access to the Father's lap 24/7. The impossibly good news is actually true: *God wants to do life with us!* In every waking moment we have an invitation to know Father intimately, to love the people in our world extravagantly, and to co-create with God in our unique calling and character. That is seriously good news.

What's more, this kingdom community grows life-on-life. By calling others into the spiritual adventure, we do life with others just as we do with God. Whatever we have learned—or are learning—we pass along to others. Or as Paul wrote it to Timothy, "The things which you have heard from me in the presence of many witnesses, entrust these to faithful men who will be able to teach others also" (2 Timothy 2:2).

This book is a collection of the core truths and practices of following Christ that I have received from others who have gone before me and that I have passed on to hundreds of other faithful men in my wake. It is my hope that you will internalize these principles in your journey, meet God in them transformationally, and then pass them to others, who will pass them to others still.

Let's recap the big ideas from our content chapters, starting with chapter two:

2. **Living the Kingdom Life**. The gospel we speak of so frequently is, in Jesus' words, really the "gospel of the kingdom." The invitation He extended to those early disciples and to us today is to "follow Me." Follow me into, not just the church community, but into the realm where I rule, the place

where Satan's power is broken, the place where I am establishing a new way of thinking and loving and living—by the very power of heaven.

3. **Jesus' Blueprint for His Church**. The community Christ is building finds its fullest expression in the church—the place where people are saved, healed, and delivered. Here we look at the five-fold leadership that God assigns as shepherds for this kingdom community and how we can implement this model in a life-giving way.

4. **Start With Theology**. The foundation is laid for how we can best understand God and relate to Him by exploring the core theologies of grace, depravity, election, regeneration, justification, sanctification, and perseverance of the saints. Basically, we're looking at where we begin in separation from God and how God bridges the gap to restore us into thriving relationship with Him...and how this begins the process of healing our relationships with others.

5. **The Power of the Gospel**. This chapter looks at three facets of gospel power: the blood of Christ that forgives us, the cross of Christ that gives us the ability to stop sinning, and the resurrection of Christ that allows us to be transformed in character into His righteousness. We access these power points through embracing our weakness and drawing from Him by faith.

6. **Forming Your Character**. This section addresses the reconstruction of our character in several aspects—brokenness as the solution to our pride, wooing as the solution to our fear, and abiding as the path to transformation. The parable of vine and branch in John 15 gives a brilliant word picture to this process. The chapter also discusses some life applications of love, rest, Holy Spirit, repentance, servanthood, and the strengthening of others.

7. **Carving out a Thriving Devotional Life**. Your devotional life is designed to be the "drop zone" where you are daily

resourced with all you need for the journey! It begins with a priority on "being with" and then leads us to an exchange of our worry, fear, and striving for the rest and acceptance of Father. Core tools and disciplines of meeting with God are outlined, including study, memorization, mediation, prayer, worship, intercession, journaling, and solitude.

8. **Tapping the Holy Spirit Fuel**. When Jesus ascended to heaven, He told His disciples to wait for an outpouring of power—an anointing far beyond just the principles of the gospel. Jesus relied completely upon the Spirit's power and guidance and set the standard for us to do likewise. Together we explore the nine spiritual gifts of 1 Corinthians 12 and are challenged to not be passive with these gifts but to eagerly desire them—to pursue both gift and Giver.

9. **Servant Leadership in Your Marriage**. Healthy marriages begin with healthy souls, and healthy souls begin with receiving God's love, breaking patterns of performance, and forgiving others. Marriage issues are character issues, and character begins by showing up, actively loving and pastoring your wife. This chapter explores the knotty issue of submission and offers "rules of engagement" for how to engage with your spouse in healthy ways.

10. **Understanding Kingdom Authority**. Our cultural history and identity as Americans is to challenge authority, but authority is important to God. When we fail to rightly relate to legitimate authorities in our lives—both divine and human—we open ourselves up to the enemy's authority. Obedience is an expression of right relationship to authority. Jesus, David, and the Centurion are offered as examples of appropriately submitting to God's rule through humans. We also look at the vital connection between forgiveness and authority.

11. **Finding Purpose and Guidance**. When it comes to figuring out our gifts and calling in the Body of Christ, it all begins with taking the role of a servant. From there we learn to

sharpen our spiritual senses to discern God's placement; this happens as we cultivate the spiritual practices, obey what we hear from God, and activate the presence of the Holy Spirit. We also learn to line up the four "harbor buoys" of Scripture, inner hearing, circumstance, and human authority to best discern the will and guidance of God in our lives.

12. **Partnering with God in Your Work**. Every person has a calling in this life, not just pastors. Calling leads us to vocation—an active expression of the kingdom of God in our work world, and we cannot partner effectively with God until we understand our place in the marketplace. God intends to show Himself as powerfully in the business world as in the church—through you. There is no retirement in the kingdom, only reassignment.

13. **Stewarding Your Kingdom Resources**. Here we explored the concept of stewardship, richly illustrated by the parable of the talents. All is God's, and we have been entrusted with managing His resources on the earth. In addition to seeing our work as worship, our time and money also serve as worship when employed in the eternal work of God. The tithe gives us the right to test God's commitment to our provision. Time, health, talents, energy, etc.—God invites us to use everything we've been given as tools in His economy.

14. **The Logistics of Discipleship**. The nuts and bolts of inviting someone else into a discipleship friendship and coaching him or her through the foundations of the spiritual life are covered. I share the essentials that I've learned about the practicalities of when, where, and how to meet together with your disciple and walk with him in the journey.

As you work with your disciple and run up against real-life challenges, use the chapter summaries above to find your way back to useful content.

In addition to the content itself, I have shared parts of my own story—how these truths and practices confronted and changed my life. How I have struggled and failed and then experienced God's power in my weakness.

Now it's your turn. Now you have the basic tools to disciple another person and walk alongside. Doing life with God and other people—it's simple, it's unassuming, and it's also radically changing our world, one precious life at a time. This is the explosive power of discipleship. It's the way of Jesus, and now it's yours.

JOIN THE MOVEMENT

Start a Group

Do you feel inspired and equipped from reading this book? If so, then I have done my job. And yet the opportunities have only just begun.

The real power in discipleship comes when we move from *addition to multiplication*. Practically speaking, this happens when we find several people who want to "do life with" God and with us and invite them into a group to go through this material together.

We've tried to make that as easy as possible by setting up an online store where you can order 10 copies of the book and save a third of the usual price. Go to **www.doinglifewith.com/product/doing-life-with-paperback-bundle/** to get your discount.

Welcome to the movement!

Jerry Daley

APPENDIX

Emotions List

Emotions are a window into the inner workings of the soul. They are not the final truth...but they represent a level of truth, a starting point. Until we can name our emotions, we cannot bring them to Jesus for His more encompassing truth and healing. So take a few minutes to scan this list and check the ones you have experienced in the last 24 hours.

☐	Absorbed	☐	Concerned
☐	Adoring	☐	Confident
☐	Afraid	☐	Confused
☐	Aggravated	☐	Contemptuous
☐	Alarmed	☐	Content
☐	Alienated	☐	Curious
☐	Amazed	☐	Defeated
☐	Ambivalent	☐	Delighted
☐	Amused	☐	Depressed
☐	Angry	☐	Disappointed
☐	Anguished	☐	Disgraced
☐	Annoyed	☐	Disgusted
☐	Anticipating	☐	Disillusioned
☐	Anxious	☐	Disliked
☐	Attracted	☐	Dismayed
☐	Awkward	☐	Disoriented
☐	Bitter	☐	Distrusting
☐	Bored	☐	Disturbed
☐	Brave	☐	Dreading
☐	Calm	☐	Eager
☐	Caring	☐	Elated
☐	Cautious	☐	Embarrassed
☐	Cheerful	☐	Enthusiastic
☐	Comfortable	☐	Envious
☐	Compassionate	☐	Exasperated

- [ ] Excited
- [ ] Exhausted
- [ ] Exhilarated
- [ ] Fearful
- [ ] Fond
- [ ] Frustrated
- [ ] Grief-stricken
- [ ] Grumpy
- [ ] Guilty
- [ ] Happy
- [ ] Hateful
- [ ] Helpless
- [ ] Hesitant
- [ ] Hopeful
- [ ] Hopeless
- [ ] Horrified
- [ ] Hostile
- [ ] Humiliated
- [ ] Hurt
- [ ] Indifferent
- [ ] Infatuated
- [ ] Inferior
- [ ] Insecure
- [ ] Insulted
- [ ] Interested
- [ ] Intrigued
- [ ] Irritated
- [ ] Isolated
- [ ] Jealous
- [ ] Joyful
- [ ] Lonely
- [ ] Loving
- [ ] Lustful
- [ ] Melancholy
- [ ] Neglected
- [ ] Nervous
- [ ] Numb

- [ ] Optimistic
- [ ] Outraged
- [ ] Overwhelmed
- [ ] Panicked
- [ ] Pleased
- [ ] Powerless
- [ ] Preoccupied
- [ ] Proud
- [ ] Rageful
- [ ] Receptive
- [ ] Regretful
- [ ] Rejected
- [ ] Relaxed
- [ ] Relieved
- [ ] Resentful
- [ ] Restless
- [ ] Repulsed
- [ ] Sad
- [ ] Safe
- [ ] Satisfied
- [ ] Scared
- [ ] Scornful
- [ ] Self conscious
- [ ] Shamed
- [ ] Shocked
- [ ] Sorrowful
- [ ] Spiteful
- [ ] Stunned
- [ ] Suspicious
- [ ] Sympathetic
- [ ] Tender
- [ ] Trusting
- [ ] Uncertain
- [ ] Uncomfortable
- [ ] Vengeful
- [ ] Weary
- [ ] Worried

For more books, resources, and inspiration on *Doing Life With*, visit **jerrydaley.com**.

ABOUT JERRY

Jerry Daley is a veteran in church planting, having spearheaded six different church plants across North Carolina and South Carolina over the years. After serving as a Captain in the US Air Force from 1964 to 1969, Jerry was called into ministry and studied at Fuller Seminary, Golden Gate Theological Seminary, and Columbia Seminary, completing the coursework (but not the dissertation) for a D.Min in 2013.

Jerry currently coaches, mentors, and trains pastoral leaders and teams (www.jerrydaley.com). If you are interested in having Jerry work with you or your team, he may be contacted through the website.

Jerry and his wife Nan have three grown children and eight grandchildren and reside in the mountains of North Carolina. His interests include physical fitness, reading, and endurance sports.

RESOURCES

If this book was useful for you, you'll want to get hold of Jerry's "mini-books" below. The Follow Series reflects a passion to uncover what it means to be a follower of Jesus in all aspects of life and ministry. As you know, "Follow me!" was and is Jesus' timeless call to men and women (Matthew 4:19). And so we seek to follow Him into thinking and acting and loving like Jesus. The Follow books are available on Amazon.com

BOOK ONE: FOLLOWING JESUS INTO THE POWER

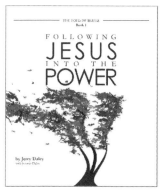

Have you ever found yourself wondering... where did all that power go?

The power to heal, physically and emotionally. The power to have the right words to say at the right time. The power to see people who are open and hungry—just like Jesus did—and lead them to the Source of Life. Is it possible for normal people to live that way too? Or was it just Jesus who got to do that stuff?

Your answer to that question changes everything! Join church-planter and leadership coach Jerry Daley on a real-world exploration to discover who the Holy Spirit wants to be in your life today. There is no reason to drift through your world powerless when Jesus' last words on earth were, "But you shall receive power when the Holy Spirit has come upon you" (Acts 1:8). It's time to power up!

BOOK TWO: FOLLOWING JESUS OUT OF THE BROKENNESS

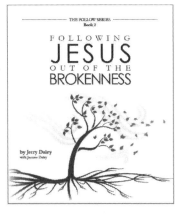

We yearn for meaning in a world marked by pain. How does the gospel lead us out of such brokenness?

Paul writes the book of Romans to describe how the gospel transforms, not just our eternal destiny, but our earthly future together. Personal suffering, relational rifts, behavioral addictions, church divisions, and even community fragmentation—all these are healed and restored by the gospel. This is Paul's promise to us. Dare we believe it?

Join church-planter and leadership coach Jerry Daley on a modern-day application of the heart of Romans to the urgent needs of local and global brokenness. Disappointment and disillusionment with the church will give way to fresh hope as we learn to not just believe the gospel, but live the gospel! Let's follow Jesus into His restoration project.

COMING TITLES

BOOK THREE: *Following Jesus Into the Blessing*
A study of the Beatitudes

BOOK FOUR: *Following Jesus Into the Freedom*
A study of Galatians

Made in the USA
Columbia, SC
26 July 2017